D0536915

haute potato

haute potato

JACQUELINE PHAM

From Pommes Rissolécs to Timbale with Roquefort, *75 Gourmet* Potato Recipes

Adamsmedia
AVON, MASSACHUSETTS

Copyright © 2013 by F+W Media, Inc.
All rights reserved.
This book, or parts thereof, may not be reproduced in any
form without permission from the publisher; exceptions are
made for brief excerpts used in published reviews.

Published by
Adams Media, a division of F+W Media, Inc.
57 Littlefield Street, Avon, MA 02322. U.S.A.
www.adamsmedia.com

ISBN 10: 1-4405-4395-X
ISBN 13: 978-1-4405-4395-1
eISBN 10: 1-4405-4396-8
eISBN 13: 978-1-4405-4396-8

Printed in the United States of America.

10 9 8 7 6 5 4 3 2 1

Always follow safety and commonsense cooking protocol while using kitchen utensils, operating ovens and stoves, and handling uncooked food. If children are assisting in the preparation of any recipe, they should always be supervised by an adult.

Many of the designations used by manufacturers and sellers to distinguish their product are claimed as trademarks. Where those designations appear in this book and Adams Media was aware of a trademark claim, the designations have been printed with initial capital letters.

Photos courtesy of Jacqueline Pham.

*This book is available at quantity discounts for bulk purchases.
For information, please call 1-800-289-0963.*

In loving memory of Baji, an extraordinary and irreplaceable woman.

Acknowledgments

To Carole, for putting up with my crazy work habits and helping me put my best foot forward. You're an amazing friend, and none of this would have happened without you. To Phoopi, Mina, Pali Apa, and Sara, thank you so much for your guidance and for teaching me how to prepare so many dishes!

To Cô Nho, thank you so much for putting up with me making a mess in the kitchen. To Ross, I'm so happy you brought this project to me! Thanks for making it happen.

And finally, to Lulu, My Girls, Daddy, and Chi Tine, you're the most supportive family I could ever have hoped for. I love you all. Thank you so much for taking care of the baby while I cooked up a storm!

contents

Chapter 6

spicy . . . 139

Chapter 7

sweet . . . 165

Introduction

Potatoes get a bad rap. They're used in popular culture to denote commonness (meat and potatoes) or laziness (couch potato). In everyday culinary use they're most often found in the form of french fries in fast-food joints, potato chips from local supermarkets, or nondescript heaps of mashed potatoes in buffet lines. But their true nature, both in the kitchen and in our culture, is far more complex and fascinating than it may seem at first blush. How many vegetables have been the subject of international public relations campaigns, or can take credit for population booms, mass migrations, political upheaval, and outright war? The humble potato can take credit for all this, and much more.

This book is my ode to the often-used but underappreciated potato. It's a celebration of the myriad culinary possibilities that are just waiting to be discovered. There are few other vegetables dynamic enough to be roasted, boiled, steamed, baked, fried, or mashed. Multiply this diversity by the dozens of varieties now readily available and the opportunity to create unique dishes truly knows no bounds. The potato is also a passport of sorts, because it allows us to sample foods and flavors from around the world. Its use in America and Europe is well documented, but elegant and exquisite potato dishes can also be found in Africa, India, and the Far East. Not surprisingly, I have found four different variations on the potato pancake alone from opposite corners of the globe. In this book I've included one of my favorites, which hails from India: a spicy potato cutlet stuffed with ground beef, or *kheema*. To illustrate the versatility of potatoes, the book is separated into chapters based on the primary flavor profile or texture of the dish. Each section is an exploration of the ways in which the potato can be used. So, though it may start its life in the ground, when combined with the right techniques and ingredients the potato can truly be haute cuisine. I hope you'll agree.

Chapter 1

refreshing

Potato dishes can often turn out greasy or heavy, but that doesn't have to be the case! Whether in starters, salads, or soups, a potato can be a bright and refreshing start to a dinner, or a perfectly balanced lunch that helps keep you going throughout the day. The key to creating light and elegant potato dishes is to select fresh ingredients that accentuate the flavor of the potato without overpowering it—citrus and green vegetables in particular are excellent options. In terms of protein, seafood pairs exquisitely with potatoes, and you'll notice that several of the recipes in this chapter make use of tuna, shrimp, and crab.

Vichyssoise

YIELDS 6 SERVINGS

Vichyssoise is a luscious soup made with potatoes, leeks, onions, a dash of cream, and vegetable stock. It was originally created by the French chef Louis Diat in 1917 at the Ritz-Carlton in New York City. He took a classic French potato leek soup from his childhood in Vichy, France, and made it summer-friendly by finishing it with cold milk.

1 pound leeks (white part only)

2 tablespoons leeks (green part only), cut into 1½" thick strips

1 tablespoon canola oil

2 tablespoons unsalted butter

1 bay leaf

2 cloves garlic, finely minced

1 pound russet potatoes, peeled and diced

1 quart vegetable stock

2 teaspoons salt

½ teaspoon white pepper, freshly ground

2 cups heavy cream

1 white onion, finely chopped

2 cups milk, cold

1. **Preparing the leeks:** Trim the hairy root but make sure not to cut so high that all the leaves separate. Cut approximately 4" off the fibrous green top of the leek and save it for garnish. Remove a layer or two if the leaves are wilted. Cut the leeks lengthwise into quarters, making sure not to cut all the way through the base, so all the leaves remain attached. Fill a large bowl of water and rinse the leeks, spreading the leaves to remove all the sand and dirt. Wash the leeks again under cold running water; chop finely.

2. **Frying the garnish:** In a heavy-bottomed small stock pot, heat the canola oil. Add the green part of the leeks. Fry until well-browned, for 3–4 minutes. Transfer to a paper towel-lined plate, leaving as much oil as possible in the pan. Set the fried leeks aside and let cool.

3. **Caramelizing the leeks:** In the same pot, add the butter to the remaining oil. Once the butter has melted, add the bay leaf, white onions, and chopped white leeks. Cook for 3 minutes, until fragrant. Add the garlic, stirring occasionally, and let the mixture cook, covered, for another 5–10 minutes.

4. **Making the soup:** Add the potatoes to the pot and deglaze with the vegetable stock. You can increase or decrease the quantity of stock, depending on how thick you want the soup. Bring to a full boil and reduce the heat to a simmer. Cook for 20–30 minutes. Remove and discard the bay leaf. Working in batches, pour into a blender (or alternatively you can just use an immersion blender directly in the pot) and pulse until very smooth. If you are using a traditional blender, allow the mixture to cool first, or else escaping

 Vichyssoise
continued

steam can blow the cover off of the machine. Strain through a mesh strainer and return to the pot. Season with salt and pepper. Add the cream and stir. Bring to a near boil. Stir well. Allow to cool to room temperature for at least 30 minutes.

5. **Assembly time:** When you're ready to serve, thin the soup with cold milk to cool the soup. Stir well. Ladle the soup into bowls. Garnish with the fried leeks.

DEGLAZING Deglazing is a cooking technique used to free the caramelized deposits of roasted or pan-fried meats and vegetables from the bottom of the pot. Any liquid, from water to vegetable stock or even wine can be used to dissolve these tasty bits and produce a flavorful sauce or soup.

Vichyssoise

Potato Frittata

Although frittatas originated in Italy, this frittata recipe is actually a variant of a Spanish dish called tortilla de patatas. *Sliced, fried potatoes are mixed with lightly beaten eggs and then cooked in a skillet. While nontraditional, the addition of yellow roasted bell peppers, hearts of palm, shallots, marinated artichokes, tarragon, and goat cheese provides a pleasing complexity to this otherwise simple breakfast fare.*

2 new potatoes

1½ teaspoons salt

1 yellow bell pepper, whole

8 whole eggs

¼ cup heavy cream

2 tablespoons milk

1 teaspoon coarse-grained mustard

2 teaspoons garlic chives, chopped

2 teaspoons fresh French tarragon, chopped

2 teaspoons chickpea flour (optional, see sidebar)

⅛ teaspoon red chili powder (or red chili flakes)

2 egg whites

¼ cup goat cheese, crumbled

3 tablespoons grape seed oil

1 shallot, thinly sliced

2 cloves fresh garlic, crushed and finely minced

1 tablespoon unsalted butter

¼ teaspoon fennel seeds (optional)

1 heart of palm, sliced

2 marinated artichoke hearts, cut into thin wedges

1 bunch green onions, chopped

4 crimini mushrooms, sliced

¼ teaspoon black pepper, freshly cracked

1 tablespoon flat-leaf parsley, chopped

1. **Boiling the potatoes:** Brush and wash the potatoes. Place them, whole and unpeeled, into a small saucepan, and fill it with cold water until the potatoes are barely covered. Bring to a boil over high heat, add 1 teaspoon salt, and reduce the heat to medium-high, cooking the potatoes for 8–10 minutes. Test with a fork; the potatoes should be slightly soft. Remove from the pot. Drain the potatoes thoroughly and let them cool a little; don't rinse them. Once the potatoes are cool enough to handle and have dried thoroughly, remove the skin. Cut them crosswise into thin ⅛" slices.

2. **Roasting the bell pepper:** Wash and dry the bell pepper, then brush with a little grape seed oil. Place a grill pan on your stovetop over high heat. Once hot, char the skin of the bell pepper, turning to evenly char the entire pepper. Wrap the hot pepper in aluminum foil; let stand for 10 minutes. Wash the pepper under running water, and the skin will come right off. Seed and thinly slice it; set aside until needed.

3. **Preparing the frittata:** In a mixing bowl, lightly beat the whole eggs with the cream and milk, until just combined. Add the mustard, chives, tarragon, chickpea flour (if using), and

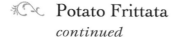

Potato Frittata
continued

red chili powder. Place the egg whites in a stainless steel mixing bowl, and add the salt. With an electric mixer, beat the egg whites for 2 minutes at medium speed. Increase to the maximum speed, and beat for another 2–3 minutes, until the whites are stiff. Do not overbeat or the texture will become grainy. Pour ⅓ of the egg whites into the frittata mixture and gently stir to soften the egg batter. Add 1 tablespoon goat cheese and the rest of the egg whites. Gently fold the mixture together with a rubber spatula. Set aside.

4. **Assembly time:** Preheat your oven to broil. In a heavy skillet, on the stovetop, heat the oil over high heat. Add the sliced potatoes and pan-fry for 2–3 minutes until lightly golden on both sides. Transfer to a plate. In the same skillet, add the shallot; cook for 5 minutes, until fragrant. Add the garlic and fennel seeds, stirring regularly, and let the shallot mixture cook for another 3 minutes until fragrant. Add the heart of palm, potato slices, bell pepper, artichoke hearts, green onions, mushrooms, and butter. Cover with a lid and cook until lightly browned, then immediately pour in the egg mixture. Season with salt. Allow to sit for 30 seconds without stirring. Delicately scrape the sides and bottom of the pan with a silicone spatula to loosen the mixture. Let it sit for 2 minutes

over medium-low heat. Sprinkle with black pepper. Set a large flat plate over the skillet and invert the frittata onto the plate. Add a little more oil to the skillet and slide the frittata back in, with the other side facing up. Allow the eggs to cook for approximately 4 minutes, without stirring, until set. Once the eggs are firm, sprinkle with the rest of the crumbled goat cheese and place under the broiler for approximately 2 minutes, or until the top is golden. Garnish with parsley. Serve immediately or at room temperature.

CHICKPEA FLOUR Chickpea flour (called *besan* in Hindi) is a common ingredient in Indian cooking—it's the main ingredient in paratha, a flat Indian bread. Here, the chickpea flour adds a delightful thickness, complexity, and body to the eggs that is hard to replace.

Coal-Cooked Sweet Potatoes with Pomegranate-Molasses Butter

YIELDS 6 SERVINGS

My family's summer season is filled with pool parties and lots of barbecues. Grilled meats and vegetables make the meal, but who doesn't love great potato side dishes as well? If you're looking to make something out of the ordinary, give this recipe a try. These potatoes will cook perfectly without a lot of effort, and they look amazing. As a bonus, sweet potatoes are much healthier than regular potatoes.

4 sprigs fresh rosemary, slightly bruised with the back of a knife

6 sweet potatoes

6 tablespoons unsalted butter, softened to room temperature

2 teaspoons blossom honey (optional)

1 tablespoon pomegranate molasses

½ teaspoon freshly ground cinnamon

⅛ teaspoon sea salt

1. **Coal-cooking the sweet potatoes:** Make sure to start with new coals; remove and discard any old ashes. When building the fire, do not use lighter fluid, since it's unhealthy to ingest. I typically use a chimney starter with some torn newspaper to get the coals nice and hot. Place the coals in a pyramid shape to provide good air circulation. After approximately 30 minutes, the coals should be ashy and gray. Once the coals are ashed over, place sprigs of rosemary on them for a nice aroma. Bury the whole, unpeeled sweet potatoes in the coals and bake them for 45 minutes, rotating the potatoes occasionally. Check for doneness. The inside should be soft without falling apart. If not done, cook for an additional 20 minutes. Remove the potatoes from the ashes. Once they're cool enough to handle, brush the ashes from the skin.

2. **Making the pomegranate-molasses butter:** Cream the butter with honey (if using). Add the pomegranate molasses, ground cinnamon, and sea salt. Transfer to a ramekin and seal with plastic wrap. Let the butter mixture stand, covered, at room temperature for 30 minutes to allow the flavors to develop.

3. **Assembly time:** Using a sharp knife, slit the sweet potatoes in half lengthwise. Serve with a pat of the pomegranate-molasses flavored butter.

Cream of Rosemary Roasted Beet and Potato Soup

YIELDS 8 SERVINGS

In France, a velouté *is a velvety soup thickened with crème fraîche. In this particular soup, I blended in potatoes and rosemary-flavored beets that are roasted until fragrant and caramelized, which give the soup an absolutely incredible color. With a garnish of rosemary-infused cream, you'll have a great first course for an elegant winter meal.*

1 pound red beets (about 8)

3 sprigs rosemary, lightly bruised

¼ cup extra-virgin olive oil

1 teaspoon salt

½ teaspoon white pepper, freshly ground

1 yellow onion, thinly sliced

1 bouquet garni (see sidebar)

2 cloves garlic, finely minced

1 quart vegetable stock (or chicken broth)

1 cup heavy cream

2½ pounds new potatoes, peeled and cut into ¾" pieces

3 tablespoons crème fraîche

1. **Roasting the beets:** Preheat the oven to 400°F. Scrub the beets under running water. Reserve any beet leaves for another dish. Place the unpeeled beets and 2 sprigs of rosemary onto a baking pan. Drizzle with 2–3 tablespoons olive oil. Season with salt and pepper, and toss to coat. Roast for 45–50 minutes. Let the beets cool completely, and discard the rosemary sprigs. Wipe the skins off using paper towels, then coarsely chop and set aside.

2. **Caramelizing the onions:** While the beets are cooking, heat the remaining olive oil in a pot. Add the sliced onions. Separate and spread the onions. Add the bouquet garni and lower the heat to medium-low. Cook for 15 minutes, until the onions become golden brown and tender. Season with salt and pepper. Add the garlic; continue stirring, and let the onion mixture cook for another 5–10 minutes. Deglaze the pan with the vegetable stock.

3. **Infusing the garnish:** Chop the remaining sprig of rosemary. Place ½ cup cream and the rosemary in a small saucepan. Bring to a near boil, then remove from the heat and let the rosemary infuse the cream. Let cool to room temperature. Transfer to a stainless steel bowl and using an electric handheld mixer, whip the cream, at low speed, for 2–3 minutes until foamy. It should be thin enough to be able to drizzle onto the soup. Season with salt and white pepper. Set aside.

4. **Making the soup:** Add the potatoes and roasted beets to the onion and vegetable stock pot. You could increase or decrease the quantity of vegetable stock, depending on how thick you want the soup. Bring to a full boil and simmer the vegetables for 20–30 minutes. Remove and discard the bouquet garni. Working in batches, place the contents of the pot in a blender. Pulse until very smooth. Strain the blended soup back into the pot. Season with salt and pepper. When you're ready to serve, add the remaining ½ cup cream and the crème fraîche, stirring well to combine. Reheat the soup for 5 minutes.

5. **Assembly time:** Ladle the soup into bowls. Top with a spoonful of the rosemary-infused cream, forming a spiral, and immediately swirl the cream using a toothpick. Garnish with sprigs of rosemary on the side.

BOUQUET GARNI The traditional bouquet garni is composed of a sprig of thyme, 2 bay leaves (torn in half), the green portion of a leek, a few curly parsley stems, and a small stalk of celery. You can always tweak the combination by substituting your favorite ingredients. To create a garni, gather all the ingredients in a large disposable tea bag or a square of cheesecloth and tie it with some twine, then use it to flavor sauces and broths.

Cream of Rosemary Roasted
Beet and Potato Soup

Salade Niçoise

YIELDS 4 SERVINGS

Salade niçoise hails from the Côte d'Azur region of France and is named after the city of Nice. This is not the tuna salad one usually finds in America, slathered in mayonnaise and sweet pickles. It's a combination of tomatoes, potatoes, green beans, eggs, and oil-packed tuna, and is typically topped with anchovies and Dijon vinaigrette.

3 heads baby butter lettuce

8 ounces *haricots verts* (French green beans)

1 dozen baby Yukon Gold potatoes, washed and peeled

1 teaspoon salt, divided

2 shallots

½ teaspoon brown sugar

3 tablespoons lemon juice

1 dozen quail eggs

1 cup black olives, sliced

2 dozen cherry tomatoes, halved

12 ounces albacore tuna fillet, shredded in small chunks

1 dozen anchovy fillets (optional)

1⅓ cups Dijon-champagne vinaigrette (see sidebar)

1 tablespoon curly parsley, finely chopped

1. **Preparing the butter lettuce:** Wash and spin dry the whole butter lettuce leaves. Set aside.

2. **Blanching the green beans:** Wash the green beans; blanch them for 4–5 minutes in boiling water and transfer into an ice bath. Drain thoroughly, then pat dry on a paper towel. Do not overcook the green beans; they should still be tender and crisp. Trim the ends of the beans, and cut into 2" long pieces. Set aside.

3. **Steaming the potatoes:** Using a pot with a steamer insert, add cold water until it barely touches the steamer. Place the peeled potatoes in the steamer and bring the water to a boil over high heat. Add ⅔ teaspoon salt, then reduce the heat to medium-high. Steam for 8–9 minutes. The potatoes should be fork-tender. Remove from the steamer, set aside, and let cool completely. Cut the potatoes into halves—or, if you prefer smaller pieces, into quarters.

4. **Pickling the shallot:** Peel and finely mince the shallot. Place the minced shallot in a bowl, sprinkle with the brown sugar and drizzle with the lemon juice. Set aside.

5. **Cooking the quail eggs:** Place the eggs in a saucepan and cover them with water. Place the pan over high heat, and as soon as the water reaches a full boil, add ½ teaspoon salt. Lower the heat to medium-low, cook for 2–3 minutes, then turn off the heat. Cover the pan with a lid and let the quail eggs sit for about 10–12 minutes. Transfer to an ice bath and cool the eggs completely. Once cool, peel and halve them.

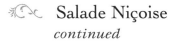
6. **Assembly time:** Use butter lettuce leaves as bowls. Place them on a serving platter. Combine all the ingredients, except the vinaigrette and parsley, and distribute the salad evenly into the lettuce bowls. Drizzle with the Dijon-champagne vinaigrette. Garnish with curly parsley.

MAKING CHAMPAGNE VINAIGRETTE

In a sealable jar, dissolve 1 tablespoon honey in 5 tablespoons champagne vinegar. Add 1 tablespoon honey mustard, salt and pepper (to taste), and whisk in ½ cup avocado oil (or other type of oil). Cover with a lid and shake well, until combined.

Salade Niçoise

Crab, Avocado, and Potato Salad in Endive Cups

YIELDS 6 SERVINGS

Shredding crab meat in a salad helps stretch the number of servings you can get out of one whole fresh crab, which is perfect when you're entertaining. Served in endive cups, this salad gets a nice color contrast from the vibrant avocado.

2 avocados

2 limes

1 yellow bell pepper

1 red bell pepper

2 tablespoons olive oil

1 whole fresh crab

2 new potatoes

1 teaspoon salt

1 teaspoon garlic chives

1 teaspoon French tarragon, finely chopped

1½ cups arugula, shredded at the last minute

1 clementine (or any sweet citrus fruit)

2 cloves pickled garlic

1 teaspoon sea salt, divided

2 teaspoons coarse-grained mustard

2 teaspoons honey

1 tablespoon dill

¼ teaspoon wasabi paste (optional)

⅓ cup avocado oil

¼ cup red onion, thinly sliced

¼ teaspoon white pepper, freshly ground

2 heads Belgian endive

1. **Boiling the potatoes:** Scrub and place the whole, unpeeled potatoes in a saucepan. Add cold water until the potatoes are barely covered. Bring to a boil over high heat, add 1 teaspoon salt, and reduce the heat to medium-high. As soon as the water boils, cook for approximately 20 minutes, until tender. Remove from the pot. Drain the potatoes thoroughly and let them cool a little, but do not rinse. Once they're cool enough to handle, cut them into ½" cubes.

2. **Preparing the avocado:** Slice the avocado in half and remove the pit. Using a mandoline or a sharp chef's knife, slice the unpeeled avocado into thick ribbons. Transfer to a plate, removing the peel for each slice. Cut the slices in half lengthwise. Drizzle with the juice of half a lime to avoid oxidation.

3. **Roasting the bell peppers:** Wash and dry the bell peppers, then brush with a little olive oil. Place a grill pan on your stovetop over high heat. Once hot, char the skins of the bell peppers, rotating to char the entire pepper. Wrap the hot peppers in aluminum foil; let stand for about 10 minutes. Wash the peppers under running water, and the skins will come right off. Seed and thinly slice them; set aside until needed.

4. **Preparing the crab:** Clean the crab, scrub with a soft brush, and rinse thoroughly. Place in a pot; add approximately 1–1½ cups of water and bring to a boil for 10–15 minutes, or approximately 8 minutes per pound. Transfer to an ice water bath for 3 minutes to stop the cooking process. Drain and discard all liquid. Remove and discard the abdominal flaps (the triangle-shaped tail). Lift and separate the back fin with the rest of the claws by using a large tablespoon at the bottom of the crab as a lever. Remove and discard the lungs (also known as devil's fingers); they have a spongy texture and are inedible. Gently remove the crab meat from the back fins. Crack the claws using a meat tenderizer mallet and gather all the crab meat in a large mixing bowl, reserving the claw meat and large crab pieces for garnish. Add the potato cubes, garlic chives, tarragon, shredded arugula, and juice of the remaining limes.

5. **Making the clementine vinaigrette:** Cut and juice the clementine. Using a strainer, remove the pulp, then place the juice in a small saucepan. Bring to a boil over high heat, then immediately lower the heat to a gentle simmer and heat for about 4 minutes. The liquid should reduce to approximately 2 tablespoons of concentrated juice. Once reduced, remove from the heat. Strain the mixture through a fine mesh sieve one more time, so the vinaigrette is clear. Place the pickled garlic in a mortar and pestle. Sprinkle with ¼ teaspoon sea salt and mash the mixture into a coarse purée, then transfer to a small bowl. Add the mustard, reduced juice, honey (if using), dill, wasabi paste (if using), and avocado oil. Whisk well. Add the red onion, and season with salt and white pepper. Let stand for at least 15 minutes to allow the flavors to develop.

6. **Assembly time:** Trim the base of the endives. Wash, dry, and separate the leaves. In a mixing bowl, combine the roasted bell peppers and crab meat. Drizzle with the clementine vinaigrette and toss lightly. Place 2–3 avocado slices into the end of each endive leaf. Using 2 teaspoons, gather a portion of the crab and round it off into an egg shape. Place the crab into the space where the pit of the avocado used to be. Place the endive cup onto a large serving platter. Repeat and fill the rest of the endive leaves with salad. Garnish with large pieces of crab and more snipped garlic chives.

Crab, Avocado, and
Potato Salad in Endive Cups

Potato and Carrot Soufflé

Individual carrot and potato soufflés are a delicious and easy dish to make if you have guests coming over for a light brunch. The soufflés can be prepared in advance and placed in the oven one hour prior to your guests' arrival. These particular soufflés are flavored with cumin, thyme, nutmeg, and smoked Cheddar cheese. Pair them with a simple arugula salad and you're all set!

1 tablespoon olive oil
2 shallots, chopped
1 white potato, peeled and diced
4 small carrots, peeled and diced
1 teaspoon salt
3 whole eggs, separated

⅛ teaspoon cayenne powder
1 cup whole milk
2 tablespoons unsalted butter, plus more to grease ramekins
1½ tablespoons all-purpose flour
1 cup smoked Cheddar cheese, grated

¼ teaspoon cumin, freshly ground
¼ teaspoon nutmeg, freshly grated
¼ teaspoon white pepper, freshly ground
¼ teaspoon cream of tartar

1. **Softening the vegetables:** Preheat the oven to 400°F. In a pot, heat the olive oil over high heat. Add the shallots and cook for approximately 3 minutes, until slightly golden. Add the potato and carrots. Sauté for 2 minutes. Add 1–1½ quarts of water. Bring to a boil and reduce the heat to a gentle simmer. Cook for 30 minutes. Once the water evaporates, check doneness (add more water if the potato or carrots aren't fully cooked and keep cooking if not yet cooked) and transfer to a platter. Season with ½ teaspoon salt and let them cool. Pass the carrots, potato, and shallots through a food mill or a potato ricer.

2. **Making the soufflé batter:** In a mixing bowl, whisk the egg yolks with the cayenne powder for 2–3 minutes. Set aside. In a small saucepan, bring the milk to a near boil. Turn off the heat and set aside. In another saucepan, melt the butter over medium-low heat, being careful not to burn it. Once the butter is hot and golden, bring the heat back up to medium-high and add the flour. Stir continuously with a whisk for approximately 3 minutes. The flour should absorb the butter and form a paste. Slowly add the milk in 3 stages. Increase the heat while constantly stirring for approximately 5 minutes. Reduce the heat to low. Add the carrot-potato mixture, Cheddar cheese, cumin, and nutmeg. Season with salt and pepper. Turn off the heat and let the mixture rest until it's time to assemble the dish. Once the mixture has cooled to room temperature, stir in the egg yolks until the texture is even, smooth, and creamy.

Potato and Carrot Soufflé
continued

3. **Assembly time:** Place the egg whites in a stainless steel mixing bowl. Add ¼ teaspoon salt and cream of tartar. Beat the egg whites for 2 minutes at medium speed. Pour ⅓ of the egg white mixture into the potato-carrot mixture and gently stir to soften the batter. Add the rest of the egg whites and, using a spatula, gently fold the egg whites into the mixture to get an airy batter. Transfer the batter to 8 small ramekins, greased with butter. Bake for 10 minutes at 400°F, then lower the temperature to 375°F and cook for another 15–20 minutes. Serve immediately.

Vietnamese-Style Shrimp and Potato Salad

YIELDS 8 SERVINGS

The flavors of this dish are drawn from the dry-roasted jasmine powder, thinly shredded fried potatoes, taro root, jicama, and onions. The whole mixture is topped with common Vietnamese salad elements, such as pickled carrots, daikon radish, chilies, Vietnamese herbs, and shrimp.

2 carrots

1 daikon radish

1¾ tablespoons salt, divided

5 tablespoons palm sugar (or granulated sugar), divided

Juice of 2 limes

1 green mango

½ English cucumber

¾ cup canola oil, as needed

1 yellow onion, peeled and sliced

½ jicama, peeled and sliced in ½" thick pieces

¼ taro root, peeled and shredded

5 Yukon Gold potatoes

1 tablespoon dried fried shallots (store-bought), optional

¼ cup jasmine rice

2 tablespoons rice vinegar

¼ teaspoon red chili powder

1 pound raw medium shrimp, thawed

1 head butter lettuce, leaves separated

1 jalapeño pepper

½ cup pickled lotus roots, drained, rinsed, and sliced

1½ cups soybean sprouts, blanched

1½ cups fish sauce dressing (see sidebar)

3 tablespoons Vietnamese spicy coriander (*rau răm*), chopped

2 tablespoons Vietnamese mint, chopped

2 tablespoons Thai basil, chopped

3 tablespoons cilantro, chopped

¼ teaspoon black pepper, freshly cracked

2 tablespoons salted roasted peanuts, coarsely crushed

1. **Preparing the carrots and daikon:** Trim the carrots and daikon on both ends. Using a mandoline, shred the carrots and daikon into 5" long thick strips. Place both ingredients in a large mixing bowl. Sprinkle with ½ teaspoon salt and 2 tablespoons sugar; drizzle with the juice of half a lime. Toss well. Let sit for about 20 minutes to draw out the moisture. Discard the juice.

2. **Preparing the green mango:** Using a sharp knife, trim the end of the mango and peel it. Shred it with a julienne vegetable peeler, or pass it through the mandoline, until you reach the pit.

Repeat the same procedure for the other side. Wrap the mango strips in plastic and chill until ready to assemble.

3. **Preparing the cucumber:** Cut the cucumber in half lengthwise. Using a spoon, remove the seeds, which will create a cavity. Slice the cucumber lengthwise into ½" slices. Layer a cooling rack on top of a cookie sheet, and place the cucumber slices on top. Sprinkle ½ teaspoon salt on both sides and let sit for at least 30 minutes. Pat dry with a kitchen towel. Cut crosswise into ½" matchsticks. Set aside.

4. **Frying the onion:** In a large nonstick pan, heat ¼ cup oil. Working in batches, add the onion in single layers and fry until golden brown for 3–4 minutes. Transfer to a platter lined with paper towels, leaving as much oil as possible in the pan. After you've drained the onion, reserve 2 tablespoons and transfer the rest to a large bowl. Add more oil between batches if necessary.

5. **Frying the jicama:** In the same large pan that you cooked the onion, add 1 tablespoon oil and fry the jicama slices until golden brown. Remove from the pan. Once they're cool enough to handle, cut the pieces into very thin strips. Set aside.

6. **Preparing the taro and potatoes:** Place the shredded taro in a large bowl. Add the juice of half a lime and cover it with ice water. Let sit for 15 minutes. Drain the taro and discard the liquid, removing as much excess water as possible. Pat dry using kitchen towels. Repeat the same procedure with the potatoes but use the juice of 1 whole lime.

7. **Frying the taro and potatoes:** In the same large pan, heat 2 more tablespoons oil. Working in batches, sprinkle 4–5 tablespoons taro evenly into the pan. Do not stir. Let stand and wait for at least 2 minutes until one side is nicely fried, crisp and golden. Flip the taro using chopsticks or a spatula and cook for another 2–3 minutes until crispy. Continue until all the taro is fried, and then repeat the same procedure with the potatoes. Add more oil between batches if necessary. Once the taro and potatoes are nicely browned, transfer to a platter lined with paper towels. As soon as all the oil is drained, transfer them to the bowl with the fried onions. Add the dried fried shallots (if using) and ½ teaspoon salt and toss well.

8. **Making the dry-roasted rice powder:** Toast the jasmine rice in a dry skillet for approximately 5–7 minutes over high heat. Stir the rice until the grains turn a rich brown color. Remove from the heat and let cool. Grind the grains into a very fine powder using a food processor or spice grinder. You could also use store-bought roasted rice powder, called *thinh*, found in any Asian specialty market, but the mill won't be as fine.

9. **Seasoning the mixture:** Add the sliced jicama to the mixing bowl. Add 2 tablespoons of the sugar and 1½ teaspoons salt, and sprinkle with the dry roasted rice powder. Toss well and set aside.

10. **Cooking the shrimp:** Combine 1 quart water, 1 tablespoon sugar, the vinegar, chili powder, and reserved fried onions in a small saucepan. Bring to a boil. Once the liquid has begun to take on some color, add the shrimp and ¾ tablespoon salt, and cook for 2–3 minutes. Check the doneness of the shrimp; they should be firm and white, with shades of orange. Drain the cooked shrimp, discarding the liquid. Once they're cool enough to handle, carefully shell and devein the black part of the shrimp using a sharp paring knife, then halve lengthwise.

11. **Assembly time:** Cover a serving platter with the leaves of lettuce. In a large mixing bowl, combine all the elements of the salad, except the shrimp, herbs, and peanuts. Drizzle with ½ cup fish sauce dressing and toss well. Add the chopped herbs. Place the salad mixture onto the lettuce, then top with the shrimp and sprinkle with coarsely crushed peanuts. Serve immediately, with the remaining fish sauce dressing on the side.

FISH SAUCE DRESSING
(NƯỚC MẮM CHẤM) To make fish sauce dressing, combine ½ cup granulated sugar and ¾ cup coconut soda, (or coconut water), in a saucepan over high heat. Boil the mixture until the sugar is dissolved, then let the liquid cool to room temperature. Add 6 tablespoons rice vinegar, 3 tablespoons freshly squeezed lime juice, 2 cloves minced garlic, and 1 finely chopped Thai red chili pepper (to taste). Finish with ½ cup first press, extra-virgin fish sauce or soy sauce, and stir well.

Vietnamese-Style Shrimp
and Potato Salad

Fava Bean and Pomegranate on Potato Bruschetta

YIELDS 8 SERVINGS

This potato antipasto replaces the traditional bread-based bruschetta with an unexpected deep-fried mixture of potatoes and bread crumbs. The refreshing topping is made with fava beans, pomegranate seeds, diced tomatoes, red onion, and basil. It's the perfect starter to an elegant dinner party.

2 pounds uncooked Pommes de Terre Chamonix dough without cheese (see Chapter 3)

1 Yukon Gold potato, peeled and shredded

Juice of 1 lemon

1 teaspoon garlic powder

½ cup bread crumbs

2 eggs

1 quart canola oil

8 ounces fava beans

¾ teaspoon sea salt

½ teaspoon black pepper

⅓ cup pomegranate seeds

2 ounces perlini-sized (pearl) fresh mozzarella cheese, drained

4 plum tomatoes, chopped

2 tablespoons red onion, finely chopped

2 tablespoons sweet basil leaves, thinly snipped

1 clove pickled garlic, finely minced

1 teaspoon white balsamic vinegar

2 tablespoons extra-virgin olive oil

1 teaspoon salt

¼ teaspoon black pepper

1. **Forming the bruschetta pieces:** Line two baking trays with silicone mats or sheets of parchment paper. Place the mashed potato dough in a piping bag with a ribbon decorating tip and pipe out 4" long sticks (about 2" wide). Make sure to space them about 1" apart so they're easy to pick up. Using your finger, flatten both ends by moistening with water. Place the trays in the freezer for about 15 minutes until the dough is firm.

2. **Preparing the potato:** Place the shredded potato into a bowl. Barely cover with a little water and the lemon juice. Let sit for 5–10 minutes. Drain the potato using a fine mesh colander; discard the liquid. Place the shredded potato in cheesecloth and remove as much excess water as possible. Pat dry with paper towels and finely chop.

3. **Breading the potato bruschetta:** Add the garlic powder and bread crumbs to the finely chopped potato. Lightly beat the eggs in a shallow bowl. Remove the potato sticks from the freezer; dip them in the egg mixture, and then coat with the finely chopped potato and bread crumb mixture.

4. **Deep-frying the bruschetta:** Line a cooling rack with paper towels and stack on top of a baking sheet. In a large Dutch oven or a deep fryer, heat 4" of canola oil for approximately 2 minutes over high heat, until the oil is slightly bubbly and a thermometer registers 345°F–360°F. Test the oil by dropping a piece of the shredded potato into the hot oil. It should sizzle. Placing one potato stick at a time in the hot oil, with up to 5 sticks per batch, deep-fry the potato bruschetta in the hot oil for 4–5 minutes per side until golden and crunchy, flipping each piece using a spider skimmer. Repeat for the remaining potato pieces. Make sure the potato sticks don't touch each other while frying. Delicately lift each potato bruschetta, draining as much oil as possible and transfer them to the cooling rack.

5. **Preparing the fava beans:** Blanch the fava beans in a quart of salted (about ¾ teaspoon salt) boiling water for 2 minutes. Drain, and immediately transfer into an ice bath. Shell the beans. Pat dry on a towel, then season with sea salt and pepper to taste.

6. **Making the topping:** In a mixing bowl, combine the fava beans, pomegranate seeds, perlini mozzarella, tomatoes, red onions, basil, and garlic. Drizzle with the balsamic vinegar and extra-virgin olive oil. Season with salt and pepper to taste.

7. **Assembly time:** Spread about 1 tablespoon of the topping on each potato piece. Drizzle with olive oil. Serve immediately.

Patates Fingerling à l'Anglaise et à l'Orange Sanguine

YIELDS 8 SERVINGS

Here's a fresh update of potato salad. Fingerling potatoes are simply boiled, then seasoned with a mint-flavored sour cream sauce. The twist is the addition of blood orange slices, which add sharp contrast of color and flavor to the dish.

4 pounds fingerling potatoes
1 tablespoon salt
2 blood oranges
1 cup sour cream
1¼ cups plain Greek-style yogurt
2 teaspoons honey

1 clove pickled garlic, finely minced
1 tablespoon sherry wine vinegar
1 6" celery stalk, peeled and sliced on the blas
1 green onion, thinly sliced
¼ cup fresh mint, thinly sliced

1½ teaspoons salt
½ teaspoon black pepper, freshly cracked
1 tablespoon walnut oil
2 tablespoons walnuts, coarsely chopped
2 tablespoons capers, coarsely chopped

1. **Preparing the potatoes:** Wash the potatoes. Place them in a pot, and fill it with cold water until the potatoes are barely covered. Bring to a boil over high heat, add 1 teaspoon salt, and reduce the heat to medium-high. Boil the potatoes for 20 minutes until slightly tender but still firm. Drain the potatoes thoroughly, without rinsing, and let them cool a little.

2. **Cutting the orange segments:** Using a sharp knife, peel the oranges and trim both ends so that the orange sits flat. With the same knife, remove the membrane wall on one side around a segment. Separate the segment along the next membrane. Free the segment and gently pull it away from the fruit, removing the membrane. Repeat and separate the remaining segments.

3. **Making the sauce:** In a bowl, combine the sour cream, yogurt, honey, garlic, vinegar, celery, green onion, and 3 tablespoons mint. Season with salt and pepper. Finish with the walnut oil and stir.

4. **Assembly time:** Cover the boiled potatoes with the sauce and toss until well coated. Garnish with walnuts, orange segments, capers, and the remaining mint leaves.

Chapter 2

decadent

Decadence can take many forms. One way to create decadent dishes is to take an everyday meal and elevate it with the right combination of ingredients. This is certainly the case with recipes such as Baked Potatoes Filled with Caviar and Tangerine Crème Fraîche Sauce or Lobster Corn Chowder. Both dishes are fairly commonplace, but it's the special additions that make them memorable.

Another important key to creating truly decadent meals is to take special care in the presentation of the dishes; luckily, potatoes can be shaped and molded into whatever form you need. They can be fried, boiled, baked, or roasted, and this versatility leads to a multitude of culinary possibilities. Pommes de Terre Fourrées aux Girolles (chanterelle-filled potato cups), for example, are a striking way to start a meal. Similarly, the Tarte Pomme de Terre (potato tart), when placed on your dinner table, is bound to elicit *oohs* and *aahs*. Between its versatility and its ability to play well with a range of exciting flavors, the humble potato is uniquely suited for extravagance, as you'll see in this chapter.

Timbale with Roquefort

YIELDS 6 SERVINGS

Timbale means "drum" in French. Timbales are a perfect choice for dinner parties because they look great, the servings are individually sized, and they can be filled with just about anything. These potato cups are packed with braised fennel, water chestnuts, and blue cheese.

3 ounces fresh water chestnuts

5 purple potatoes

1¾ teaspoons salt

4 tablespoons unsalted butter, softened to room temperature

1 clove garlic, halved and lightly crushed

½ cup heavy cream

1 fennel bulb

3 tablespoons olive oil

2 shallots, thinly sliced

1 jalapeño pepper, roasted, skinned, seeded, and finely chopped (see sidebar)

1 tablespoon fresh dill, chopped

⅛ teaspoon nutmeg, freshly grated

¼ teaspoon black pepper, freshly ground

2 ounces Roquefort, crumbled

1. **Cooking the water chestnuts:** Wash the chestnuts in cold water and then soak them in lukewarm water for about 30 minutes. With a paring knife, make a small crisscross cut at the root of each water chestnut; don't cut down to the flesh. Place the chestnuts in a pot and cover them with water. Bring to a gentle boil and cook for 30 minutes. Allow to cool. As soon as you can handle them, shell the water chestnuts, then slice and cut them into small matchsticks. Set aside.

2. **Parboiling the potatoes:** Brush and wash the potatoes. Place them, whole and unpeeled, into a large pot, and fill it with cold water until the potatoes are barely covered. Bring to a boil over high heat, add 1 teaspoon salt, and reduce the heat to medium-high, cooking the potatoes for 6–8 minutes. Test with a fork; the potatoes should be slightly tender but still firm. Remove from the pot. Drain the potatoes thoroughly and let them cool a little; don't rinse them. Once the potatoes are cool enough to handle and have dried thoroughly, remove the skin. Cut them crosswise into thin ¼" slices.

3. **Making potato cups:** Line 6 ramekins with parchment paper. Grease the paper with a thin layer of butter and rub garlic on the bottom and inner sides of each ramekin. Pour about 1½ teaspoons cream into the bottom of each dish. Finely mince the garlic, and set aside. Place the potato slices along the sides of the ramekins, using the parchment paper as a liner against the wall of the molds. Fill the gaps and bottom of the mold with more sliced potatoes. Using a smaller round tin cake mold, gently press the potatoes into the

bottom and sides of the ramekin. Retain enough sliced potatoes for the tops of the cups.

4. **Preparing the fennel:** Discard the stalk of the fennel bulb, reserving the fronds for garnish. Cut the bulb into ¹⁄₁₆" thick slices using a mandoline or a sharp chef's knife. In a nonstick pan, heat the olive oil over high heat. Add the garlic and fry for about 2 minutes until golden. Transfer to a small bowl and set aside. In the same pan, add the shallots. When the color is lightly golden, add the roasted jalapeño pepper and the sliced fennel. Cook for 5–7 minutes, until slightly browned. Season with remaining salt. Add the water chestnuts and 2 teaspoons dill. Mix well; lower the heat and cook for another 2–3 minutes. If the mixture starts sticking to the bottom of the pan, add ¼ cup water. Transfer to a bowl. Set aside.

5. **Assembly time:** Preheat the oven to 375°F. In a small bowl, combine the heavy cream, fried garlic, nutmeg, salt, and pepper. Fill the ramekins with a layer of the fennel mixture. Sprinkle about ½ teaspoon Roquefort. Drizzle about 1 teaspoon of the cream mixture. Repeat the same procedure for an additional layer. Cover the top with sliced potatoes. Sprinkle the tops with the remaining

cheese. Place in the oven and bake for 10 minutes at 375°F; lower the heat to 350°F and continue baking for another 35–40 minutes. Remove from the oven, and check the tenderness of the potatoes with a knife. Allow to cool for at least 15 minutes. Gently remove the potato timbales from the ramekins. Discard the parchment paper. Garnish with dill, the fennel fronds, and the sauce of your choice.

ROASTED JALAPEÑO PEPPERS

Once you know how to make them yourself, you'll never buy the ones in a jar again. To start, discard the stem; wash, pat dry, and brush with canola oil. Place a grill on your stove and char all the skin of the pepper. Remove it from the heat, and then wrap the pepper in aluminum foil. Allow to cool for 5–10 minutes. Clean the pepper with a knife; the skin will come right off. Seed the pepper and finely chop the flesh. But be sure not to rub your eyes after handling jalapeño peppers!

Timbale with Roquefort

Pommes Rissolées

YIELDS 8 SERVINGS

Pommes rissolées are a French classic. They're crisp, cube-shaped, pan-fried potatoes flavored with herbs. The secret ingredient in this recipe is duck fat, which gives a unique body and richness. Ground saffron and a hint of cayenne pepper add color; they're nontraditional additions but really enhance the final result. You know the saying: You eat with your eyes first!

2 sprigs French tarragon

16 Yukon Gold potatoes

3 teaspoons salt

½ cup duck fat, as needed

2 cloves garlic, halved lengthwise

1 teaspoon saffron (optional), finely ground with a mortar and pestle

1 teaspoon cayenne pepper (optional), as needed

1 teaspoon white pepper (or black pepper), freshly ground

2 tablespoons garlic chives, finely snipped

2 tablespoons flat-leaf parsley leaves, finely chopped

1 **Preparing the tarragon:** Remove the tarragon leaves from the stems: Hold the top of the stem with one hand and slide the other hand along the stem, pulling the leaves off. Slightly bruise the leaves in a mortar and pestle to release the flavor. Finely chop the bruised herbs. Set aside.

2. **Parboiling the potatoes:** Wash the potatoes. Place them whole and unpeeled into a large pot. Fill it with cold water until the potatoes are barely covered. Bring to a boil over high heat; add salt and reduce the heat to medium-high, boiling for 10–12 minutes. Test, using a fork; the potatoes should be slightly tender but still firm. Drain the potatoes thoroughly and let them cool a little. Once the potatoes are cool enough to handle and have dried (with no excess water),

carefully remove the skin. Dice them into ¼" cubes.

3. **Browning the potatoes:** Preheat the oven to 200°F. Divide the diced potatoes into 4 batches. In a large nonstick pan, melt 2 tablespoons duck fat over high heat. Add ½ clove of garlic and the first batch of potatoes. Reduce the heat to medium-high. Cover the pan loosely with a sheet of aluminum foil, and cook for 3–4 minutes. Do not move the potatoes until the bottoms are fully browned, then toss frequently (but gently) with a silicone spatula. Sprinkle the crisp potatoes with the chives and parsley, ¼ teaspoon ground saffron (if using), ¼ teaspoon cayenne pepper (if using), and ¼ teaspoon pepper. Add more duck fat if needed, and cook for another 3–4 minutes, continuing to toss well. Check for

doneness of the potatoes. They should be crispy on the outside and soft on the inside. Transfer them onto a duck fat–greased baking pan, and immediately season with ½ teaspoon salt. Keep warm in the oven while the rest of the batches of potatoes are being browned. In between each batch, clean the pan with a paper towel, then add more duck fat and another half clove of garlic. Repeat the same procedure for each batch.

4. **Serving the potatoes:** Just before you're ready to serve, sauté the potatoes one more time in the pan. If needed, keep warm in the oven until you're ready to serve. Serve hot.

Tarte Pomme de Terre

YIELDS 6 SERVINGS

The concept of a tarte salée *(French for "savory pie") is pretty simple. The flaky dough is made with puff pastry and the filling is usually made from vegetables with a cheese topping. Potatoes work wonderfully, both in terms of taste and texture. The filling for this potato pie is made of a layer of caramelized onions, tomato sauce, pan-fried potatoes, and a cheese topping.*

1 pound frozen puff pastry dough (store-bought)	1½ teaspoons salt	3 tablespoons canola oil, as needed
2 tablespoons olive oil	1 14-ounce can basil and tomato sauce	½ teaspoon paprika (or red chili powder)
1 yellow onion, finely chopped	1 teaspoon honey (optional)	¼ cup Gruyère cheese, thinly sliced
2 shallots, finely chopped	2 teaspoons herbes de Provence (see sidebar)	1 tablespoon garlic chives, snipped
1 tablespoon unsalted butter	½ teaspoon black pepper, freshly cracked	¼ cup crème fraîche
1 clove fresh garlic, finely minced	10 Yukon Gold potatoes	

1. **Preparing the tart shell:** Make sure the puff pastry dough is thawed, but still cold. Using a rolling pin, roll the dough into a 12" × 15" rectangle. Place the dough in a nonstick rectangular 8" × 12" tart mold lined with parchment paper; following the curve of the mold, crimp the dough against the edge. Gently press the dough with your fingers so there are no air bubbles. Leave a little excess above the edge to account for shrinkage. Prick the dough all over with a fork. Chill in the refrigerator for 20–30 minutes. Line the dough with another sheet of parchment paper, and top with ceramic pie weights or dried beans. Place the tart mold on a baking sheet and bake for 12–14 minutes. Remove the pie weights and discard the parchment paper. Bake for another 2–3 minutes, so the pie crust can dry. Remove from the heat and let the crust cool a little. Set aside.

2. **Caramelizing the onions:** In a large nonstick pan, heat the olive oil over medium heat. Add the onion and shallots and cook until they're shiny, stirring frequently to prevent them from burning. Add the butter and garlic, and season with salt. Cook until golden, approximately 5–7 minutes. Transfer ⅔ of the onions to a plate, leaving as much oil as possible in the pan.

3. **Making the tomato sauce:** Add the tomato sauce, honey (if using), and herbes de Provence to the remaining onions in the pan. Cook for 10 minutes, or until the mixture is thickened and spreadable. It should become almost like a paste.

Adjust seasoning to taste. Transfer to a bowl and set aside.

4. **Parboiling the potatoes:** Brush and wash the potatoes. Place them whole and unpeeled in a large pot. Fill with cold water until the potatoes are barely covered. Bring to a boil over high heat, add 1 teaspoon salt, and reduce the heat to medium-high, boiling the potatoes for 10–11 minutes. Test with a fork; the potatoes should be slightly tender but still firm. Remove from the pot. Drain the potatoes thoroughly and let them cool a little, without rinsing. Once the potatoes are cool enough to handle and have dried thoroughly, cut them into ½" thick slices.

5. **Browning the potatoes:** Divide the sliced potatoes into 2 batches, or more if needed. In the same pan that you cooked the onion and sauce in add the canola oil over high heat. Add the first batch of potatoes, but don't overcrowd the pan. Reduce the heat to medium-high. Pan-fry for 2–3 minutes. Using a silicone spatula, flip the potatoes. Cook the other side for another 2–3 minutes until nicely browned. Season with paprika, salt, and pepper. Check for doneness; they should be crispy on the outside and soft on the inside. Adjust seasoning. Set aside. Repeat the process

with each batch until all the potatoes are browned on both sides.

6. **Assembly time:** Preheat the oven to 375°F. Fill the tart shell with the caramelized onion filling, then spread on a layer of tomato sauce. Add the Gruyère cheese and chives. Top with the pan-fried potatoes. Bake at 375°F for 8 minutes. If necessary, to ensure the potatoes are browned, change the setting to broil for about 2 minutes. Remove from the oven and garnish with more chives. Allow to rest for at least 10 minutes. Serve warm or at room temperature.

HERBES DE PROVENCE Herbes de Provence is a combination of herbs originating from the Mediterranean region. They're ideal for grilled meat, tomato sauce, and ratatouille. You can create your own if you have the following ingredients: savory, fennel, basil, thyme, rosemary, and lavender.

Pommes de Terre Fourrées aux Girolles

YIELDS 4 SERVINGS

Stuffing roasted potatoes with chanterelle mushrooms makes a fantastic two-in-one potato side dish. First, potatoes are parboiled, then carved as the receptacle for the filling, and finally roasted in the oven. You could use any flavor combination for the filling. This version is made with a four-cheese tomato sauce and sautéed chanterelle mushrooms. The trick is to use waxy potatoes, which keep their shape and remain firm. These potatoes will come out beautifully!

2 tablespoons extra-virgin olive oil

1 bay leaf

1 shallot, thinly sliced

3 cloves garlic, finely minced

1 28-ounce can plum tomatoes, drained and slightly crushed

2 teaspoons light brown sugar (optional)

2 tablespoons ricotta cheese, at room temperature

2 tablespoons fontina cheese, freshly grated

2 tablespoons aged Asiago cheese, freshly grated

2 tablespoons Parmesan cheese, freshly grated

1 tablespoon salt, to taste

¼ teaspoon black pepper, freshly cracked

8 medium-size red-skinned potatoes

4 tablespoons unsalted butter, melted

1 pound fresh chanterelle mushrooms, cleaned and patted dry

2 tablespoons white wine (or white wine vinegar)

1½ tablespoons curly parsley, finely chopped

1. **Making the four-cheese tomato sauce:** Heat the oil in a saucepan over low heat. Add the bay leaf and shallot. Cook over low heat for approximately 5 minutes, stirring frequently to prevent the shallot from burning, until the color is evenly golden brown. Increase the heat to high and add the garlic, cooking until golden. Add the tomatoes and brown sugar. Cover; decrease the heat to medium-low and simmer for 30 minutes, stirring frequently until the mixture thickens. Add the 4 cheeses. Remove and discard the bay leaf. Using an immersion blender at low speed, blend the sauce until smooth. Season with salt and pepper.

2. **Parboiling the potatoes:** Wash the potatoes; do not peel them. Cut them crosswise into 2½" thick slices and place them in a small pot. Add enough cold water to barely cover the potatoes. Bring to a boil over high heat, add 1 teaspoon salt, and reduce the heat to medium-high. Boil for 20 minutes. The potatoes should be fork-tender but still firm. Remove from the pot. Drain the potatoes thoroughly and let them cool a little.

3. **Roasting the potatoes:** Preheat the oven to 375°F. Once the potatoes are dried and cool enough to handle, select the 8 thickest slices and create a small cavity at the top of each slice, using a melon baller. Brush all sides of the potato pieces with melted butter and season with salt. Line a baking pan with a sheet of parchment paper, and place the potatoes onto the baking pan. Roast for 20–25 minutes, until slightly golden.

4. **Cooking the mushrooms:** Depending on the size of the chanterelle mushrooms, cut them in half if necessary. Add the mushrooms and the remaining melted butter from the potatoes to a pan. Sauté until shiny and well coated with butter. Add 2 tablespoons white wine and cook 2 more minutes. Add the parsley. Remove from the heat and transfer the mushrooms to a bowl. If there's any liquid at the bottom of the pan, it can be added to the tomato sauce to enhance its flavor.

5. **Assembly time:** Fill the potatoes with tomato sauce and top with the mushrooms. Serve immediately.

STORING TOMATO SAUCE You can store the leftover tomato sauce in the freezer for future use. Pour the sauce into small bags, vacuum-seal them and then place in the freezer.

Baked Bacon and Quail Eggs in Roasted Potato Cups

YIELDS 8 CUPS

Here's a simple and elegant breakfast or brunch idea. Just bake quail eggs in pre-roasted potato cups and flavor them with a little cream, garlic, pecorino cheese, French tarragon, and bacon. It's a great way to wake up your taste buds in the morning!

4 red-skinned potatoes
Juice of 1 lemon
2 teaspoons salt
4 tablespoons unsalted butter, melted
1 tablespoon olive oil
2 cloves garlic, finely minced

8 quail eggs
2 tablespoons heavy cream, as needed
½ teaspoon black pepper, freshly cracked
1 tablespoon bacon bits
1 teaspoon French tarragon, finely chopped

1 tablespoon curly parsley, finely chopped
¼ cup pecorino cheese, freshly grated

1. **Preparing the potatoes:** Wash and peel the potatoes. Cut them crosswise into 2" thick slices. Place them in a small pot. Add the lemon juice and enough cold water to barely cover the potatoes. Bring to a boil over high heat, add 1 teaspoon salt, and reduce the heat to medium-high, boiling for about 30 minutes. The potatoes should be fork-tender but still firm. Remove from the pot. Drain the potatoes thoroughly and let them cool a little. Once the potatoes are cool enough to handle, create 8 potato cylinders using a $^{37}/_{16}$" (88-millimeter) scalloped-edged circle cutter, or any similarly sized circle cutter. Depending on the size of the potatoes, you might be to able make more cylinders.

2. **Carving the potato cups:** Preheat the oven to 375°F. Create a small cavity at the top of each cylinder, using a melon baller. Brush all sides of the potato pieces with melted butter and season with salt. Line a baking pan with a sheet of parchment paper. Place the potatoes onto the baking pan, and roast for 10–15 minutes.

3. **Assembly time:** In a small saucepan, heat the oil over medium heat. Add the garlic and fry for 2 minutes until fragrant and golden. Set aside. Open the oven and transfer the hot baking pan to a workspace. Divide and add the fried garlic into each potato cup, then crack an egg into each potato cup. Drizzle with about ¾ teaspoon cream. Season with salt and pepper. Add bacon bits, herbs, and a sprinkle of cheese. Return to the oven and bake for 10–12 minutes. Allow the cups to cool for at least 15 minutes. Serve warm.

Baked Bacon and Quail Eggs
in Roasted Potato Cups

Crêpes Vonnassiennes with Smoked Salmon

YIELDS 28 SERVINGS

Miniature appetizers are perfect for dinner parties; they allow people to nibble without interrupting the flow of conversation. In this recipe, mini crêpes vonnassiennes are topped with smoked salmon and crème fraîche and tied with a knot of fresh dill. They taste as delicious as they look; these bite-sized potato "blinis" are always a hit.

¾ cup crème fraîche

1 teaspoon ginger, freshly grated

2 teaspoons garlic chives, finely snipped, and extra for garnish

2 tablespoons lemon juice, freshly squeezed

2 teaspoons lemon zest

1 teaspoon Himalayan pink salt (or regular salt)

1 tablespoon horseradish mustard

3 Yukon Gold potatoes

1½ teaspoons salt, as needed

3 tablespoons all-purpose flour, sifted

⅛ teaspoon turmeric

3 whole eggs

1 teaspoon granulated sugar

¼ teaspoon cayenne pepper (optional)

½ teaspoon black pepper, freshly ground

3 egg whites

¼ cup olive oil

¼ bunch fresh dill, with its stems

4 slices smoked salmon, cut into 2" wide slices

1. **Making the lemon crème fraîche sauce:** In a bowl, combine the crème fraîche, ginger, chives, lemon juice and zest, and horseradish mustard. Season with ½ teaspoon pink salt.

2. **Preparing the potatoes:** Scrub the potatoes. Place them whole and unpeeled in a large pot. Fill it with cold water until the potatoes are barely covered. Bring to a boil over high heat, add 1 teaspoon salt, and reduce the heat to medium-high. Boil the potatoes for approximately 20 minutes, until slightly tender but still firm. Drain the potatoes thoroughly, without rinsing, and let them cool a little. Once the potatoes are dried and cool enough to handle, remove the skin and grate them using the largest holes of a box food grater. Transfer to a large mixing bowl.

3. **Making crepes:** Mix the shredded potatoes with the flour and turmeric and set aside briefly. Using an electric handheld mixer, whisk the 3 whole eggs with the sugar until the texture becomes thick. Add the cayenne pepper (if using). Season with salt and pepper. Add the egg mixture to the shredded potatoes. Add ⅛ teaspoon salt to the egg whites, and beat them for 2 minutes at medium speed. Increase to maximum speed and keep beating for another 2–3 minutes until the whites are stiff. Pour ⅓ of the beaten egg whites into the potato mixture and gently stir everything to soften the batter. Pour in the rest of the egg

whites and, using a spatula, gently fold them in to get an airy batter.

4. **Cooking the crêpes:** Place a flat nonstick or cast-iron griddle over medium heat. When the griddle is hot, brush with a thin layer of oil and, in batches, add 1-tablespoon mounds of the batter. You can cook 6–7 crêpes at a time, depending on how much space you have. Using the back of a spoon, even out the thickness of the pancakes to about ¼" thick. Lower the heat to medium-low. Let the crêpes cook for 1–2 minutes, without moving them. When you see the edges start to dry and get firm, take a small flat spatula and lift around the edges; they should be golden. Flip them over and cook for another minute until browned. Transfer to a cooling rack lined with paper towels. Repeat the same procedure until all the batter is used.

5. **Softening the dill stems:** Reserve a few sprigs for garnish. Quickly blanch the remaining long stems of dill by dipping them for 7–8 seconds in boiling water, then transferring to an ice bath.

6. **Arranging presentation:** Even out the edges of the crêpes using a 2" diameter circle cutter, so the appetizers are the same size. Wrap a slice of salmon around the circle cutter. Gently secure the salmon with a dill stem, and tie the stem around the salmon, holding it in place. Carefully remove the circle cutter, leaving behind a ring of salmon. Repeat the same procedure for the rest of the salmon slices.

7. **Assembly time:** Place the mini crêpes vonnassiennes on a large serving platter. Top each with a ring of salmon. Spoon or pipe the lemon crème fraîche sauce into the salmon rings. Cover the dill knots with fresh dill and garnish with chives. Finish with a sprinkle of grated Himalayan pink salt.

Baked Potatoes Filled with Caviar and Tangerine Crème Fraîche Sauce

Do you have a favorite baked potato recipe? This one is simple, yet very sumptuous, with the luxurious delicacy that is caviar. The trick to making this dish really pop is to pair the caviar with a refreshing sauce. The combination of tangerine and crème fraîche works perfectly.

10 new potatoes	1 teaspoon tangerine zest	Himalayan pink rock salt, freshly grated (or regular salt)
⅓ cup coarse sea salt	1 teaspoon maple syrup (optional)	
¾ cup crème fraîche	¼ cup caviar	
2 tablespoons tangerine juice, freshly squeezed	1 tablespoon fresh dill	

1. **Baking the potatoes:** Preheat the oven to 400°F. Scrub the potatoes and pat them dry. Prick the skin all over with a small, sharp knife for faster cooking time. Spread the sea salt onto a baking sheet, and place the potatoes on the salt. Bake for 40 minutes until soft, starchy, and tender. Once the potatoes are cool enough to handle, use a small, sharp knife to slit a large cross at the top side of each potato, cutting halfway down. Using your thumb and index finger, gently but firmly squeeze and push the potato flesh through the opening. Clear the opening a little, by hollowing out a bit of the center. Set some of the filling aside. Let cool completely to room temperature.

2. **Preparing the tangerine crème fraîche sauce:** In a bowl, combine the crème fraîche, tangerine juice, zest, and maple syrup (if using). Season with ¼ teaspoon pink salt.

3. **Assembly time:** Spoon a dollop of the sauce into the potatoes. Top with the caviar and garnish with fresh dill. Grate a little pink salt over the potatoes. Serve immediately.

Baked Potatoes Filled with Caviar
and Tangerine Crème Fraîche Sauce

Prosciutto-Wrapped Fig and Gnocchi Bites

YIELDS ABOUT 4 DOZEN APPETIZERS

In this recipe, gnocchi are paired with figs, then wrapped in prosciutto and, finally, baked until crispy. The contrast of textures and flavors from the salty baked prosciutto and the warm, chewy gnocchi is a true adventure for the palate.

1¾ pounds white potatoes	1 teaspoon black pepper	3 dozen figs
1 tablespoon kosher salt (or regular salt), divided	1¾ cups all-purpose flour	12 slices prosciutto, sliced into quarters
2 eggs	10 tablespoons olive oil, divided	1 bunch sweet basil leaves, as needed
¼ teaspoon nutmeg	2 tablespoons butter, diced	

1. **Boiling the potatoes:** Brush and wash the potatoes, then place them whole and unpeeled in a large pot. Fill it with cold water until the potatoes are barely covered. Bring to a boil over high heat, add 1 teaspoon salt, and reduce the heat to medium-high. Boil the potatoes for 25–30 minutes, until slightly tender but still firm. Drain the potatoes thoroughly, without rinsing, and let them cool a little. Once the potatoes are dried and cool enough to handle, remove the skin and mash them with a potato masher. Set the mashed potatoes aside to cool to room temperature.

2. **Forming the gnocchi:** In a bowl, lightly beat the eggs with a fork. Add the nutmeg and season with salt and pepper. Form a well in the center of the cooled mashed potatoes and pour in the egg mixture. Reserving 2 tablespoons, add the remainder of the ½ cup flour. Mix until the batter is smooth, but do not overmix. Add 7–8 tablespoons oil and the reserved flour, and knead the dough until it becomes a smooth ball. Roll the dough into 4 1¼" diameter, 16" long logs. Using a paring knife, cut the logs into 1¼"-long pieces. Smooth the edges and form oval-shaped ball pieces. Flatten the gnocchi ¼" thick, then join the extremities that are the most distant from each other by overlapping the 2, rolling into a ball again with a small slit. Dust the formed gnocchi with flour.

3. **Boiling the gnocchi:** Bring 3 quarts of water to boil over high heat. Add the gnocchi, bring back to a boil, and then immediately lower the heat to a gentle boil. Cook the gnocchi for 3–4 minutes, until they float to the surface. Salt the water halfway through the cooking process with 1 teaspoon of salt, and stir gently but constantly, so the gnocchi don't stick to the bottom. When the gnocchi are cooked, reserve ⅓ cup pasta water, and drain the gnocchi, but do not rinse. Let stand in a colander.

4. **Sautéeing the gnocchi:** In a large nonstick sauté pan, heat 2 tablespoons oil over high heat. Add the gnocchi and butter at the same time. Toss the gnocchi by moving the pan in a circular motion. When the gnocchi have a golden outer crust, season with 1 teaspoon salt and ½ teaspoon pepper. If the pasta starts sticking to the bottom, add some of the reserved pasta water. Transfer to a large serving platter. Separate the gnocchi and let cool for at least 10 minutes before assembling the appetizers.

5. **Preparing the figs:** Preheat the oven to 400°F. Using kitchen shears, make a cross incision starting from the stem of the figs, cutting three-quarters of the way to the root. Open up the figs like a flower.

6. **Assembly time:** Line 4 baking sheets with silicone mats or sheets of parchment paper. Insert a gnocchi into each fig, place 2 basil leaves against the figs and then wrap a prosciutto strip all the way around the fruit. Secure with a party pick. Place the wrapped figs on the baking sheets, making sure to space the prosciutto bites about 1"–2" apart. Bake for approximately 15 minutes until

crispy. Remove from the oven and allow to cool for at least 20 minutes. Serve warm with your favorite refreshing dipping sauce or fruit chutney.

FIG SUBSTITUTE Depending on the season, you can use fresh figs or dried figs. For other delicious options, you can replace the figs with apricots, pitted cherries, or dried plums, wrapping them tightly to the gnocchi.

Prosciutto-Wrapped Fig
and Gnocchi Bites

Goat Ricotta and Chorizo Filled Hash Browns

YIELDS 2 SERVINGS

Here's an upscale version of hash browns with a surprise goat ricotta and chorizo center. The chorizo adds a little spiciness to the dish without overpowering the hash browns, and also adds some protein. The goat cheese has a tang and a velvety texture that complement the other components of the dish quite well. There's nothing wrong with good old-fashioned hash browns, but if you're in the mood for something a little different, this is a great recipe to try.

2 Yukon Gold potatoes
1 tablespoon lemon juice
1½ tablespoons jasmine rice flour
½ yellow onion, thinly sliced

2½ tablespoons goat ricotta cheese
1 tablespoon onion chives, finely snipped
¾ teaspoon salt

¼ teaspoon white pepper, freshly ground
3 tablespoons canola oil, as needed
6 teaspoons chorizo

1. **Preparing the potatoes:** Wash and peel the potatoes, then shred them and place them in a bowl. Barely cover the potatoes with cold water and add the lemon juice. Let sit for 5–10 minutes. Drain the potatoes using a fine mesh colander. Discard the liquid. Place all the shredded potatoes in a cheesecloth and remove as much excess water as possible, then pat dry with paper towels. Sprinkle the rice flour over the potatoes; toss well. Add the onion, goat ricotta cheese, and 2 teaspoons chives. Season with salt and pepper. Mix well.

2. **Assembly time:** In a heavy-bottomed skillet, heat the oil over high heat until hot. Grease disposable gloves with oil, then form flattened patties with the potato mixture. Lower the heat to medium-high, and place the patties in the skillet.

Add a teaspoon of chorizo in the center of each hash brown patty. Cover the chorizo with a few more shreds of potato. Brown the hash browns for approximately 3 minutes, then gently flip the hash browns using a spatula. Cook for another 2–3 minutes, until golden. Transfer the hash browns onto a large platter lined with paper towels. Garnish with chives. Serve immediately with some ketchup on the side, if you like.

Goat Ricotta and Chorizo
Filled Hash Browns

Pommes de Terre Farcies à la Viennoise

YIELDS 6 SERVINGS

This is the recipe for twice-baked Viennese-style potatoes. The filling consists of crème fraîche, Emmentaler cheese, eggs, and herbs, such as chervil, chives, tarragon, and parsley. They make ideal appetizers for a buffet-style party or as one of the main elements of a festive brunch.

6 russet potatoes
½ cup sea salt
6 tablespoons unsalted butter, diced
2 whole eggs
½ teaspoon granulated sugar

¼ teaspoon cayenne pepper
2 teaspoons flat-leaf parsley, chopped
2 teaspoons chervil, chopped
2 teaspoons French tarragon, chopped
2 teaspoons garlic chives, chopped

½ teaspoon nutmeg, freshly grated
¾ cup crème fraîche
10 ounces Emmentaler cheese, grated
¼ teaspoon black pepper, freshly cracked

1. **Preparing the potatoes:** Preheat the oven to 400°F. Scrub the potatoes; pat them dry. Prick the skin all over with a small, sharp knife for faster cooking time. Spread the sea salt onto a baking sheet, then place the potatoes on top of the salt. Bake for 1 hour and 15 minutes, until soft and tender. Once the potatoes are cool enough to handle, create little "hats" by cutting on the long sides of the potatoes, the tops off the oval potatoes. Using a melon baller, create a cavity by hollowing out the center of the potatoes, creating approximately ¼" thick potato shells. Place the scooped-out flesh in a mixing bowl and add 3 tablespoons of the butter. Using the back of a fork, mix until well combined.

2. **Making the filling:** Using an electric hand-held mixer, whisk the eggs with the sugar until the texture becomes thick. Add the cayenne pepper (if using), herbs, nutmeg, and crème fraîche.

Add the egg mixture to the potatoes. Mix well. Add 7 ounces of the Emmentaler cheese. Season with salt and pepper.

3. **Assembly time:** Melt the rest of the butter. Remove and discard the sea salt from the baking sheet. Grease the baking sheet with the melted butter. Brush the skin of the emptied potato shells with melted butter and arrange them flesh side down on the baking sheet. Bake for 4–5 minutes. Open the oven, turn the potato shells upright and brush the insides with more melted butter. Return to the oven for another 2–3 minutes. Take the baking sheet out of the oven and fill the potato skins with the herb-potato mixture. Top with the remaining Emmentaler. Return to the oven and change the setting to broil; brown for approximately 2 minutes, until the cheese is melted and there's a golden crust. Serve immediately.

Pommes Château with Fried Calamari, Basil, and Tomato Cherry Relish

YIELDS 8 SERVINGS

This side dish is fit for a king! Potatoes are cut into small cylinders and sautéed in butter. Once crispy and golden, they're covered with cherry tomatoes, dried sour cherries, and fried calamari, three exciting tastes which play off of the backdrop of the potatoes. These edible pieces of art are almost too pretty to eat!

3 pounds Yukon Gold potatoes

¼ cup olive oil, as needed

1 tablespoon kosher salt (or regular salt)

1½ teaspoons white pepper, freshly ground

¼ cup oil-cured black olives, pitted and coarsely chopped

10 tablespoons rice flour

1 teaspoon garlic powder

⅛ teaspoon cayenne pepper

⅛ teaspoon turmeric

1 pound fresh baby calamari

2 cups safflower oil (or any vegetable oil)

½ bunch sweet basil leaves

1 tea bag Earl Grey tea

½ cup dried sour cherries

1 pound cherry tomatoes

1 teaspoon freshly grated ginger

2 teaspoons orange blossom honey

1 clove pickled garlic, puréed

2 tablespoons champagne vinegar

1 tablespoon curly parsley, finely chopped

1 shallot, very thinly sliced

¼ teaspoon pink peppercorns, freshly cracked

1. **Parboiling the potatoes:** Scrub the potatoes. Place them whole and unpeeled in a large pot. Fill it with cold water until the potatoes are barely covered. Bring to a boil, add 1 teaspoon salt, and reduce the heat to medium-high. Cook for about 8 minutes. The potatoes should still be firm. Drain the potatoes thoroughly and let them cool a little tle. Once the potatoes are cool enough to handle, remove the skin. Using a decorative cylinder cutter, cut them into 1½"-long cork-shaped pieces.

2. **Browning the potatoes:** Preheat the oven to 400°F. Divide the cork-shaped potatoes into 3 batches. In a large, heavy-bottomed skillet, heat 2 tablespoons olive oil over high heat. Add the potatoes in batches, making sure not to overcrowd the skillet. Reduce the heat to medium-high. Loosely cover the pan with a sheet of aluminum foil. Cook for 3–4 minutes. Using a silicone spatula, gently flip the potatoes. Cook the other side for another 3–4 minutes, until nicely browned. Season with 1 teaspoon salt and ½ teaspoon white pepper and set aside. Repeat with the other batches, adding more oil if necessary until all the potatoes are browned on both sides. Place the potatoes in a greased baking dish and finish cooking them in the oven for 15 minutes. Check for doneness; they should be crispy on the outside and soft on

the inside. Adjust salt and pepper to taste. Add
the olives, toss well, and keep warm in the oven
at 200°F until ready to assemble.

3. **Frying the basil and calamari:** In a small
bowl, combine the rice flour, garlic powder, cayenne pepper, and turmeric. Stir well. Pat the calamari dry, and season with ½ teaspoon salt and ½
teaspoon white pepper. Toss with the rice flour
mix, making sure they're well coated. Meanwhile,
line a cooling rack with paper towels and stack on
top of a baking sheet. In a small saucepan, heat
safflower oil for about 2 minutes over high heat;
there should be at least 3 inches of oil in the pan.
Once the oil is slightly bubbly, and a thermometer
registers 345°F–360°F, place one basil leaf at a
time in the hot oil and fry for 30 seconds. Using a
slotted spoon, transfer to the cooling rack. Once
the basil leaves are fried, place 4–5 calamari per
batch in the same hot oil and deep-fry for 45 seconds over high heat, until crunchy. Lower the
heat to medium, wait for another 30 seconds or
so, and delicately lift them with a spider skimmer,
draining as much oil as possible, and transfer to
the cooling rack. Repeat the same procedure for
the rest of the calamari, placing one at a time in
the hot oil.

4. **Making the tomato cherry chutney:** Make
1 cup Earl Grey tea. Soak the cherries in the cup
of hot tea to infuse for at least 15 minutes. Strain
and reserve the cherries; discard the liquid. In a
small saucepan, barely cover the cherries with
cold water. Bring to a boil, then add the cherry
tomatoes. Blanch them for 30 seconds, drain, and
transfer to an ice bath to stop the cooking process. Remove and discard the tomato skin. Cut the
tomatoes in half. In a bowl, combine the ginger,
honey, garlic, and champagne vinegar. Stir well.
Add the cherry tomatoes and their juice, the tea-
infused cherries, parsley, and shallot. Drizzle with
2 tablespoons olive oil. Season with ½ teaspoon
salt and white pepper, to taste. Allow the flavors
to combine for 15 minutes.

5. **Assembly time:** Transfer the château potatoes to a serving platter. Spoon the tomato cherry
relish over the potatoes, with as little liquid as
possible. Spread the fried calamari and fried basil
leaves over the dish. Serve immediately.

Pommes Château with Fried Calamari,
Basil, and Tomato Cherry Relish

Lobster Corn Chowder

Sumptuous and luscious would both be appropriate words to describe this soup. Lobster adds a touch of elegance to the usually down-home chowder, and the addition of corn and diced potatoes gives this soup a true stick-to-your-ribs heartiness. Even though soup is generally served as a first course, this is substantial enough to be a main dish!

2 whole live lobsters	8 cups chicken stock	1½ pounds white potatoes, peeled and cut into 2" pieces
1 cup white wine	3 tablespoons unsalted butter	¾ teaspoon white peppercorns, freshly ground
2½ teaspoons salt	¾ cup all-purpose flour	
¼ cup olive oil	½ cup whole milk, warmed	1 tablespoon curly parsley, finely chopped
1 sprig fresh thyme	1¼ cups heavy cream, warmed	
3 yellow onions, chopped	1 pinch red chili flakes, to taste	
5 corn ears, halved	¼ teaspoon turmeric	

1. **Poaching the lobsters:** Before you begin cooking, place the lobsters in the freezer for 30 minutes. Clean the lobsters; brush and rinse thoroughly. Place 1 gallon of water and ½ cup white wine (if using) in a pot. Bring to a boil. Add the lobsters to the pot, cover with a lid, and cook for 10–12 minutes. Remove from the pot and let the lobsters cool a bit. Once they're cooled enough to handle, cut each lobster in half lengthwise. Gather and reserve the coral from the head in a small bowl and discard the sand pocket near the head. Shell the claws and tails, reserving the shells and 1 quart lobster water. Pat the lobster claws and tails dry using paper towels. Cut into large pieces. Sprinkle with ½ teaspoon salt. Set aside and chill in the refrigerator until ready to assemble.

2. **Making the broth:** In a large stock pot, heat 2 tablespoons oil over high heat. Add the whole sprig of thyme and onions and cook for 10 minutes until golden and fragrant. Transfer to a plate, leaving 1 tablespoon of sautéed onion in the pot. Add the lobster shells and coral, and sauté for 2–3 minutes. Add the corn ears and cover with 1 quart of the lobster water. Cover and cook over high heat for 12 minutes. Add the chicken stock and remaining white wine if using. Allow to simmer for 30 minutes. Remove the ears of corn from the broth and set aside. Strain the broth through a fine sieve. Discard any solids. Once the corn is cool enough to handle, stand it on end and slice the kernels down with a sawing motion. You'll have about 3¾ cups corn. Coarsely mash the corn using a mortar and pestle or a few pulses in a food processor.

Lobster Corn Chowder
continued

3. **Making the *roux*:** In the same pot, melt the butter over medium-low heat. Add the flour. Keep stirring with a whisk for 2 minutes until it's well incorporated and forms a thick paste. Add the warmed milk and 1 cup heavy cream. Increase the heat, stirring constantly for 2–3 minutes. Lower the heat to low. Add the corn, reserved onions, red chili flakes, and turmeric. Cook for another minute, then add the broth. Bring the mixture to a boil and continue cooking, stirring occasionally, for approximately 10 minutes. Using an immersion blender, pulse the soup 2–3 times, so the texture is smooth.

4. **Assembly time:** Add the potatoes to the soup. Season with 2 teaspoons salt and ¾ teaspoon pepper. Cook for another 20 minutes until the potatoes are tender. Finish with the reserved cooked lobster and the remaining heavy cream; stir well. Adjust seasoning to taste. Garnish with parsley. Serve warm with bread on the side.

Lobster Corn Chowder

Chapter 3

cheesy

In several cuisines, potatoes and cheese seem meant for each other. In France, gratins come from every region and always highlight the local produce and cheese. I've included Salsify, Potato, and Cheese Gratin, one of my personal favorites. There is also a tartiflette recipe from the Haute-Savoie region of France, and the quiche, which can serve up just about any combination of ingredients. Eastern Europe presents very different, but equally delicious, potato and cheese combinations, such as cheese and potato-filled "cigars" and pierogies. I've also included a couple of recipes that are my own creations, including a gnocchi lasagna, where the pasta sheets are made from potato gnocchi dough!

Cheesy Potato Croquette Appetizers with Harissa Sauce

YIELDS 26 APPETIZERS

The word croquette *comes from the French verb* croquer, *which means "to bite, with a crisp crunch." It describes any moist, shaped item that is breaded and then pan-fried. Stuffing the croquettes with mozzarella cheese gives them a hot and gooey filling that contrasts wonderfully with the breaded crunch of the exterior. Serve the croquettes with harissa-flavored ketchup and you'll have fantastic appetizers for your next dinner party.*

1¼ pounds Yukon Gold potatoes
¼ cup canned garbanzo beans, drained
½ cup frozen peas
1 teaspoon dry mustard powder
1 teaspoon ground coriander
¾ teaspoon garlic powder

¾ teaspoon onion powder
½ teaspoon ground celery seeds
1 teaspoon paprika
1 teaspoon salt
1 8-ounce buffalo mozzarella cheese ball, as needed

1½ cups homemade bread crumbs (see sidebar)
½ cup peanut oil (or regular vegetable oil), as needed
¼ cup harissa
¾ cup ketchup

1. **Parboiling the potatoes:** Scrub and place the whole unpeeled potatoes in a small pot. Add cold water until the potatoes are barely covered. Bring to a boil over high heat, add 1 teaspoon salt, and reduce the heat to medium-high. Boil the potatoes for 10–15 minutes, until tender when pierced with a fork. Remove from the pot. Drain the potatoes thoroughly and let them cool a little, but do not rinse. Once the potatoes are dried and cool enough to handle, gently remove the skin with a paring knife and grate them using the largest holes of a box food grater.

2. **Preparing the garbanzo beans:** Using the back of a fork or a mortar and pestle, mash the garbanzo beans into a thick paste.

3. **Seasoning the potatoes:** Combine the grated potatoes and mashed garbanzo beans in a large mixing bowl. Add the green peas, mustard, ground coriander, garlic and onion powders, celery seeds, and paprika. Mix well, then divide and form approximately 26 potato balls.

4. **Preparing the potato croquettes:** Cut the mozzarella into small cubes. Insert a cube of mozzarella inside each potato ball. Reshape and completely cover the piece of cheese with potato. Set aside. Fill a flat plate with bread crumbs, then roll and coat the croquettes in the bread crumbs.

5. **Pan-frying the croquettes:** Line a cooling rack with paper towels and place on top of a baking sheet, to drain the croquettes after frying. Meanwhile, heat the oil over high heat in a large Dutch oven or any shallow pan. For a nice golden color, heat the oil until it's slightly bubbly. Test the oil by sprinkling some bread crumbs into it. They should sizzle but shouldn't turn brown too quickly. In batches, place the potato croquettes in the oil; reduce the heat to medium, and deep-fry them for 3–4 minutes until golden, rotating the pieces so all sides are crispy. Using a spider skimmer, lift each croquette, draining as much oil as possible and transfer to the cooling rack. Continue the process with each croquette batch.

6. **Assembly time:** In a small bowl, combine the harissa and the ketchup. Fill a large serving bowl lined with parchment paper with the potato croquettes and serve with the spicy ketchup on the side. Serve warm, so the cheese stays melted.

HOMEMADE BREAD CRUMBS   Use 4 pieces leftover pita bread, baguette, or sliced white bread. If the bread is still soft, place in the toaster until toasted and dried. Cut the bread into small pieces. Place in a mini food processor and grind into a fine powder. Add ¼ teaspoon paprika, ¼ teaspoon cayenne pepper, ½ teaspoon garlic powder, salt and pepper. Pulse until mixed.

Pommes Duchesse Fourrées au Fromage

YIELDS 8 SERVINGS

The name may sound fancy, but pommes duchesse are simply baked mashed potato balls. They're crunchy on the outside and soft on the inside, and ooze delightful goodness. Not only are they a perfect dish for formal events, but they dress down as well. If not fancily piped, they're named "baroness potatoes" instead (in reference to a lower rank of nobility).

4 russet potatoes
1½ teaspoons salt
7 tablespoons unsalted butter
4 egg yolks
½ teaspoon sugar
⅛ teaspoon nutmeg

2 teaspoons fresh dill, finely chopped, plus more for garnish
2 teaspoons French tarragon, finely chopped
1 tablespoon garlic chives, finely snipped
2 tablespoons bread crumbs

10 tablespoons heavy cream
¾ teaspoon white pepper, freshly ground
3 ounces mozzarella cheese, diced
1 whole egg

1. **Preparing the mashed potatoes:** Preheat the oven to 400°F. Peel the potatoes and place them in a pot, then fill it with cold water until the potatoes are barely covered. Bring to a boil over high heat, add ½ teaspoon salt, and reduce the heat to medium-high. Cook for 20–23 minutes. The potatoes should be fork-tender. Remove from the pot, then drain the potatoes and let them cool. Once the potatoes are cool enough to handle, mash them, using a food mill. Stir in 6 tablespoons butter. Set aside.

2. **Making duchess potatoes:** In a mixing bowl, beat the 4 egg yolks with the sugar for 2–3 minutes. Add the nutmeg and the egg yolk mixture to the mashed potatoes. Stir well. Add the herbs, bread crumbs, and 6 tablespoons heavy cream, and mix well. Season with ½ teaspoon salt and ½ teaspoon pepper. Put the mashed potato mixture into a piping bag fitted with a large star tip. Pipe small dots of potato two inches apart onto silicone mat–lined baking pans. Top each swirl of potato with a cube of cheese; immediately pipe more potato in an upward spiral motion and form small, golf ball–sized shapes with the cheese in the center. Wrap the trays in plastic, and place them in the freezer for about 15 minutes, or until firm. (If you plan to bake the pommes duchesse at a later time, once hardened, transfer them to a sealable bag and place back in the freezer. In this case, let the potatoes rest for about 30 minutes to room temperature before baking.)

ᶎℭᴗ Pommes Duchesse Fourrées au Fromage
continued

3. **Making the egg wash:** Using a fork, beat
the whole egg with 2 tablespoons heavy cream.
Lightly brush the egg wash over the potatoes.
Make sure to coat the entire outer surface.

4. **Assembly time:** Bake for 10 minutes, then
turn the oven down to 375°F, rotate the tray, and
bake for 10 more minutes, or until golden brown.
At the end of 20 minutes, if the potatoes are not
golden brown, change the oven setting to broil for
2 minutes. Garnish with more fresh herbs, and
serve immediately.

Spinach Gnocchi Lasagna

YIELDS 6 SERVINGS

Spinach lasagna has all the elements of a classic comfort food. It's creamy, rich, and packed with flavor. The twist in this recipe is that the pasta sheets are made of homemade potato gnocchi. Sautéed spinach in garlic is sandwiched between the pasta sheets, and a rich cheese sauce (sauce Mornay) is generously applied to the dish to bring all the ingredients together.

12 ounces homemade potato gnocchi dough (see Chapter 2, Prosciutto-Wrapped Fig and Gnocchi Bites)

¾ cup all-purpose flour, plus 2 cups for dusting

2½ teaspoons salt, to taste

¼ cup olive oil, divided

18 ounces fresh baby spinach

8 tablespoons unsalted butter, at room temperature

1 onion, thinly sliced

4 cloves garlic, finely chopped

5 cups milk, warmed

1½ cups mozzarella cheese, shredded, or more to taste

⅛ teaspoon nutmeg, freshly grated

¼ teaspoon black peppercorns, freshly cracked

1 8-ounce can tomato sauce

3 tablespoons ricotta cheese

2 tablespoons curly parsley, finely chopped

1. **Making the lasagna sheets:** Divide the dough into 10 portions. The dough should be neither too sticky nor too dry. Dust a flat work space, or cutting board, with a generous amount of flour. Roll out each ball (about 4"), then pass through a pasta machine attachment, using the widest setting to create sheets that are approximately 3" × 7". Dust the sheets with a little flour to prevent them from sticking to the machine. Keep the sheets separated and let them dry a little for at least 30 minutes on large trays dusted with flour before boiling them.

2. **Cooking the lasagna sheets:** Place 2" of water in a shallow roasting pan and bring to a boil over high heat. Using 2 large spatulas, transfer the gnocchi sheets to the boiling water. Bring back to a boil, then immediately lower the heat to a gentle boil. Cook the pasta for about 3 minutes total, until the sheets float to the surface. Salt the water halfway through the cooking process (about 1 teaspoon). When the lasagna sheets are cooked, carefully drain the liquid. Transfer the sheets to a flat surface lined with a cheesecloth and pat dry. In a large pan or wok, add 2 tablespoons olive oil. When the oil is hot, add 2 lasagna sheets at a time. When the pasta sheets have a golden outer crust, season with ¼ teaspoon salt. If the pasta starts sticking to the bottom, add some of the reserved pasta water. Transfer to a large platter and repeat the same procedure for the rest of the lasagna sheets.

3. **Preparing the spinach:** Wash the spinach thoroughly in a large bowl of water. Drain, then remove the excess water using a salad spinner. Roughly chop the spinach leaves. Wipe clean the wok and add 2 tablespoons olive oil over medium heat; add the onion. Cook for 8–10 minutes, until caramelized. Transfer the onion to a bowl and set aside. Add the garlic to the same pan. Cook for 1 minute. Keep the temperature at a high heat. Add ⅓ the amount of spinach to the pan, and toss constantly using a slotted spoon. The leaves will start to wilt after 30 seconds or so. Add ¼–½ cup water, then add the next ⅓ of the spinach as soon as the first ⅓ leaves are wilted and there's room in the pan and repeat the same procedure for 30 seconds. Season with ½ teaspoon salt to prevent the spinach from changing color. Repeat one more time with the rest of the spinach, then transfer the contents of the pan onto a large platter. Reserve the excess spinach liquid in a separate bowl. You can use the liquid to thin the Mornay sauce later if it starts to thicken too much.

4. **Making the Mornay sauce:** In a saucepan, melt 8 tablespoons butter over medium-low heat. Bring the heat back up to medium-high, and once the butter is hot and golden, add the ¾ cup flour. Stir manually with a whisk for approximately 3 minutes. The flour should absorb the butter and form a paste. Add the milk in 3 stages, and stir well until fully incorporated. Increase the heat to high while constantly stirring for approximately 5 minutes. Reduce the heat to low. Add 1 cup mozzarella cheese and the nutmeg. Season with ½ teaspoon salt and ¼ teaspoon pepper. The consistency of the Mornay sauce should be creamy and thick. Add the spinach liquid to thin the sauce.

5. **Assembly time:** Preheat oven to 375°F. In a 10" × 14" × 3" rectangular pan lined with aluminum foil and sprayed with oil, spread a layer of caramelized onions first and the can of tomato sauce, then layer up to 4½ sheets of the lasagna, depending on the size of your pan. Spread with a layer of spinach, then sprinkle with ricotta cheese. Spread about 2–3 ladles of the Mornay sauce, then add another 4½ sheets lasagna. Repeat until all the ingredients are used. Finish with the remaining Mornay sauce. Cover with ½ cup mozzarella cheese and place in the oven for 30 minutes at 375°F, until golden brown. When it's cooked, remove the pan from the oven and let it rest for at least 20 minutes. Cut into squares and garnish with parsley.

Spinach Gnocchi Lasagna

Pine Nut, Chèvre, and Potato Cigars with Lemon Caper Sauce

YIELDS 14 APPETIZERS

These baked cigars are rolled appetizers, filled with zesty goat ricotta cheese, pine nuts, and potatoes. They're a vegetarian's delight: The layers of phyllo dough provide a crispy texture, while the goat ricotta cheese creates a luscious, creamy filling that contrasts with the crunch of the pine nuts. To highlight the flavors in the filling, the cigars are served with a creamy lemon, caper, and goat ricotta cheese sauce.

3 whole eggs

1 teaspoon granulated sugar

½ teaspoon cayenne pepper

¼ teaspoon nutmeg, freshly grated

3 cups goat ricotta cheese

2 teaspoons garlic powder

2 teaspoons salt

½ teaspoon black pepper, freshly ground

2 Yukon Gold potatoes

3 tablespoons pine nuts, lightly toasted

1 Meyer lemon, zested and freshly squeezed

3 tablespoons flat-leaf parsley, chopped

½ cup fontina cheese, freshly grated

¼ cup chèvre, diced, at room temperature

2 tablespoons olive oil

¼ cup milk

¼ teaspoon turmeric

14 sheets phyllo dough, store-bought

4 tablespoons unsalted melted butter, as needed

2 tablespoons roasted sesame seeds

1½ cups lemon caper sauce (see sidebar for recipe)

1. **Boiling the potatoes:** Wash and place the whole, unpeeled potatoes in a small pot. Add cold water until the potatoes are barely covered. Bring to a boil over high heat, add 1 teaspoon salt, and reduce the heat to medium-high. As soon as the water reaches a boil, cook for 10–15 minutes, until tender. Remove from the pot. Drain the potatoes thoroughly and let them cool a little, but do not rinse. Once the potatoes are cool enough to handle and have dried completely, gently remove the skin with a paring knife and grate them using the largest holes of a box food grater. Gather 1 cup grated potatoes.

2. **Making the ricotta cheese filling:** Using a handheld mixer, whisk 2 eggs with the sugar. Add the cayenne pepper and nutmeg. In a mixing bowl, soften the goat ricotta cheese with the egg mixture into a smooth paste-like consistency. Season with garlic powder, turmeric, salt, and pepper. Add the grated potato, pine nuts, lemon zest, lemon juice, 2 tablespoons parsley, fontina cheese, chèvre, and 1 tablespoon oil. Set aside. If the texture is too dense, you can smooth it with up to 4 tablespoons milk.

3. **Working with the phyllo dough:** Preheat the oven to 375°F. Lightly grease a baking pan lined with a sheet of parchment paper. Brush a sheet of phyllo dough with a thin layer of melted butter. Fold the phyllo dough square into a triangle. Place a small mound of the potato ricotta cheese filling (about 3 tablespoons) at the base of the triangle. Moisten one of the corners with water, and fold the triangle from one corner to the midpoint of the base. It should just cover the filling. Roll the phyllo dough from the base towards the top corner. Repeat with the other corner that is along the same base. Moisten the exposed top corner with water using your finger, then finish rolling. Transfer to the baking pan and cover with a damp cloth. Repeat until all the phyllo sheets are used.

4. **Assembly time:** Once you're ready to bake, prepare the egg wash. Using a fork, beat the remaining egg with 2 tablespoons melted butter. Brush the pastries with the egg wash. Sprinkle with the sesame seeds, and chill in the refrigerator for approximately 15 minutes prior to baking. Bake for 5 minutes at 375°F, then lower the temperature to 350°F and cook for another 20 minutes, until golden and crispy. Remove from the oven and allow to cool at least 10 minutes. Serve with lemon caper sauce on the side.

LEMON CAPER SAUCE In a bowl, combine 1 cup goat ricotta cheese, ⅓ cup goat milk (or regular cow's milk), 1 teaspoon lemon zest, the juice of 1 Meyer lemon, 2 tablespoons coarsely chopped capers, and 1 tablespoon extra-virgin olive oil. Season with salt and pepper to taste.

Pine Nut, Chèvre, and Potato Cigars with Lemon Caper Sauce

Smoked Salmon Tartiflette

Tartiflette is a rich and hearty Savoyard dish (from the Haute-Savoie region of France), usually served after a long day of skiing in the French Alps. It's the ultimate cheesy potato dish, made with properly ripe Reblochon cheese. The most traditional form calls for lardons *(salted cured pork), but this version, made with smoked salmon, is lighter and equally delicious!*

4 tablespoons duck fat, at room temperature
1 clove garlic
3 tablespoons cream
2½ pounds Dutch yellow potatoes
1½ teaspoons salt

1 yellow onion, thinly sliced
1 shallot, thinly sliced
¾ cup dry white wine
1 8-ounce package sliced smoked salmon, coarsely chopped
⅓ cup crème fraîche

1 7-ounce wheel very ripe Reblochon cheese
¼ teaspoon white pepper, freshly cracked

1. **Greasing the dishes:** Grease 6 mini gratin dishes with a thin layer of duck fat, then rub garlic on the bottom and inner sides of the dishes. Pour about 1½ teaspoons cream in the bottom of each dish.

2. **Boiling the potatoes:** Peel the potatoes, cut them into 2" chunks, and place them in a large pot. Fill it with cold water until the potatoes are barely covered. Bring to a boil, add 1 teaspoon salt, and reduce the heat to medium-high, so that the potatoes don't fall apart. Cook for 20–25 minutes. The potatoes should be fork-tender. Remove from the pot and drain; allow the potatoes to cool, until they can be handled. Cut into 1" thick slices.

3. **Caramelizing the onion and shallot:** Heat 1 tablespoon of the duck fat in a large, heavy-bottomed skillet over medium-high heat. Sauté the onion and shallot over low heat for 8–10 minutes, stirring frequently, until the color is evenly golden brown and the onion and shallot are tender. Season with salt. Add the diced garlic and cook for 2 minutes, until slightly golden. Leaving as much fat as possible in the skillet, transfer to a platter and set aside.

4. **Browning the potatoes:** Divide the sliced potatoes into 4 batches. In the same skillet, add more duck fat (about 1 tablespoon). Cook the potatoes in batches, being sure not to overcrowd the skillet. Cook for 3–5 minutes, then gently flip with a silicone spatula. Cook the other side for another 3 minutes, until lightly golden. Season

Smoked Salmon Tartiflette
continued

with salt and ¼ teaspoon white pepper and set aside the first batch. Repeat with the other batches until all the potatoes are cooked on both sides. Once all the potatoes are cooked, return them all into the skillet. Add the caramelized onion and pour in the wine. Cover and simmer for 8–10 minutes. Transfer to a mixing bowl.

5. **Assembly time:** Preheat oven to 450°F. Add the crème fraîche and smoked salmon to the onion potatoes. Toss well. Adjust seasoning to taste. Transfer the mixture to the gratin dishes. Trim and remove a bit of the rind (essentially the edges of the cheese, which can be hard) from the edges of the Roblochon cheese. Cut the Roblochon lengthwise in half, then slice each half into thirds. Top each gratin dish with the piece of cheese. Place the gratin dishes in the oven for 10 minutes until golden. Check for doneness of the potatoes; they should be tender. Lower the oven to 200°F and let the potatoes stand until ready to serve.

Smoked Salmon Tartiflette

Potato Quiche Lorraine

YIELDS 8 SERVINGS

Jalapeño cheddar cheese, bacon, leeks, and small asparagus spears form the base of the filling for this delightfully tasty potato quiche. Pair the potato quiche with a green salad, and you'll have a healthful, tasty, light meal. If you make individual quiches, they can also work well as the first course of an elegant dinner.

1 pound small asparagus spears

1 14" diameter frozen tart shell (store-bought)

3 tablespoons olive oil

1 shallot, thinly sliced

1 5" piece leek (green part only), thinly sliced on the bias

2 red-skinned potatoes

4 ounces sliced bacon, chopped into small pieces

1½ teaspoons salt

¼ teaspoon black pepper, freshly cracked

2 whole eggs, separated

¼ teaspoon cayenne pepper

⅔ cup heavy cream

⅔ cup milk

¼ teaspoon nutmeg, freshly grated

1 tablespoon unsalted butter

¼ teaspoon cream of tartar

12 ounces jalapeño Cheddar cheese, grated

1. **Parboiling the potatoes:** Brush and wash the potatoes. Place them whole and unpeeled in a large pot. Fill with cold water until the potatoes are barely covered. Bring to a boil over high heat, add 1 teaspoon salt, and reduce the heat to medium-high, boiling the potatoes for 10–11 minutes. Test with a fork; the potatoes should be slightly tender but still firm. Remove from the pot. Drain the potatoes thoroughly and let them cool a little, without rinsing. Once the potatoes are cool enough to handle and have dried thoroughly, cut them into ½" thick slices.

2. **Trimming the asparagus:** Trim about ½" from the root of each asparagus, then cut them in quarters. Place in the freezer until ready to assemble.

3. **Making the tart shell:** Preheat the oven to 375°F. With a rolling pin, roll the dough between 2 sheets of parchment paper and place into a 9" diameter pie pan lined with one of the parchment paper sheets. Following the curve of the mold, crimp the dough against the edge. Gently press the dough with your fingers so there are no air bubbles. Leave a little excess above the edge, because the dough will settle a bit in the oven. Prick the dough all over with a fork. Chill in the refrigerator for 20–30 minutes. Line the dough with another sheet of parchment paper and top with ceramic pie weights or dried beans. Place the pie pan on a baking sheet and bake for 10 minutes. Remove the pie weights and discard the top parchment paper, then bake for another 5 minutes so the pie crust can dry. Remove from the

oven and let the crust cool a little. Make sure the crust is not cracked. If so, patch the crust with more dough. Set aside.

4. **Making the quiche filling:** In a large, non-stick pan, heat 2 tablespoons olive oil over high heat. Add the sliced shallot and leek. Cook until shiny, stirring frequently to prevent them from burning. Transfer to a plate and let cool to room temperature. Add 1 tablespoon oil to the pan, if all of the oil has been absorbed. When the oil comes back up to temperature, add the potatoes and bacon. Cook for 5–7 minutes, and season with ¼ teaspoon each of salt and pepper. Let cool and transfer the bacon, potatoes, and asparagus to the tart shell. Set aside.

5. **Making the quiche batter:** In a mixing bowl, whisk the egg yolks with cayenne powder for 2–3 minutes. Add the shallot, leek, cream, milk, and nutmeg. Place the egg whites in a glass or stainless steel mixing bowl, and add ¼ teaspoon salt and cream of tartar. With an electric beater, beat the egg whites for about 2 minutes at medium speed, until frothy. Pour ⅓ of the egg white mixture into the egg yolk mixture and gently stir to soften the batter. Add the rest of the egg whites

and gently fold the egg whites into the egg yolks with a spatula.

6. **Assembly time:** Fill the pie shell with the quiche batter. Cover with the Cheddar cheese. Bake for 30 minutes at 375°F. Rotate the quiche and bake for another 10 minutes until the egg mixture is set and the top is golden. A small knife or a toothpick inserted into the quiche should come out clean. Remove from the oven, and allow to cool for at least 20 minutes, or to room temperature, before serving.

Potato Quiche Lorraine

Papaya, Stilton Cheese, and Shiitake Mushroom Potato Skins

YIELDS 8 SERVINGS

The soul of these appetizers is grilled shiitake mushrooms mixed with caramelized papaya. The mixture is nestled in a crispy potato skin and smothered in gooey Stilton cheese. The strong flavor from the cheese complements the natural sweetness from the papaya. This dish is a great example of how the fusion of cultures and flavors can work.

8 russet potatoes
⅓ cup coarse sea salt
2 tablespoons olive oil
8 shiitake mushrooms, quartered
   lengthwise

1 tablespoon curly parsley, chopped
1 tablespoon dried fried shallot (store-
   bought, optional)
½ ripe papaya, peeled, seeded, and
   chilled

2 tablespoons unsalted butter, diced
¼ teaspoon black pepper, freshly cracked
1½ cups mild white Stilton cheese,
   crumbled

1. **Baking the potatoes:** Preheat the oven to 400°F. Scrub the potatoes and pat them dry. Prick the skin all over with a small, sharp knife. Spread the sea salt onto a baking sheet, then place the potatoes on top of the salt. Bake for 1 hour and 15 minutes, until soft and tender. Once the potatoes are cool enough to handle, cut the tops off the oval side of the potatoes. Using a melon baller, create a cavity by hollowing out the center of the potato. Create 8 ¼"-thick potato shells. Reserve half the amount of scooped-out flesh in a bowl and stir in 1 tablespoon butter. Store the remaining potato flesh in the refrigerator for up to 2–3 days for another use.

2. **Grilling the mushrooms:** Preheat a grill pan. Brush the pan with olive oil over high heat. Lightly coat the mushrooms with oil, using a silicone brush. Place the shiitakes on the grill, and cook for 2 minutes on each side. They should be soft, but should still hold their shape. Remove from the heat and transfer the mushrooms to the potato bowl. Add parsley and the fried shallots. Set aside.

3. **Caramelizing the papaya:** Make sure the papaya is chilled. Pat the papaya pieces dry with paper towels, then brush with olive oil. Place the papaya on the hot grill for 2–3 minutes per side, until grill marks have formed. Remove from the heat, then sprinkle with ½ teaspoon sea salt. Cut the papaya into cubes. Add the papaya and its juice in the potato bowl and stir.

4. **Assembly time:** Remove and discard the sea salt from the baking sheet. Arrange the emptied

Papaya, Stilton Cheese, and Shiitake Mushroom Potato Skins
continued

potato shells on the clean baking sheet, flesh side down. Bake for 4–5 minutes. Open the oven, turn the potato shells upright and brush the insides with 1 tablespoon melted butter. Return to the oven for 2–3 minutes. Remove the potatoes from the oven; fill the potato skins with the potato mixture, then top with crumbled Stilton. Return to the oven and change the setting to broil; brown for approximately 2 minutes, until the cheese is melted and there's a golden crust. Serve immediately.

DRIED FRIED SHALLOTS   You can find dried fried shallots at Asian specialty stores. They're crunchy and very strong in flavor. You can also make your own by frying thinly sliced shallots, if you like. In a large pan, heat 4 tablespoons canola oil. Once the oil is hot, add 2 thinly sliced shallots in a single layer and fry until golden brown. Transfer to a platter lined with paper towels, leaving as much oil as possible in the pan.

Salsify, Potato, and Cheese Gratin

YIELDS 6 SERVINGS

Salsify gratin is a very common French winter dish that makes use of the root of the salsify plant, which has a flavor reminiscent of oysters. For this version, steamed fingerling potatoes and diced Granny Smith apples make the flavors more interesting, with the acidity of the apples and the starchiness of the potatoes giving the salsify a great balance in both texture and taste. The Mornay sauce for this gratin is made with Cheddar cheese, and the crust is topped with rich, nutty Dubliner cheese, which takes this classic French version of comfort food to another level of richness.

1 8.8-ounce can salsify, drained	1 teaspoon white pepper, freshly ground	1 cup milk, warm
6 fingerling potatoes	4 tablespoons butter	¼ cup aged yellow Cheddar, diced
2 teaspoons salt	2 tablespoons curly parsley, finely chopped	⅓ cup Dubliner cheese, shaved
2 tablespoons olive oil	1 teaspoon thyme, finely chopped	⅛ teaspoon nutmeg, freshly grated
2 shallots, finely chopped	1 teaspoon marjoram, finely chopped	2 teaspoons honey Dijon mustard
1 Granny Smith apple	1½ tablespoons flour	
Juice of 1 lemon		

1. **Preparing the salsify:** Blanch the salsify vegetables for 30 seconds in boiling water, drain, and pat dry on a paper towel.

2. **Steaming the potatoes:** Using a pot with a steamer insert, add cold water until it barely touches the steamer. Place the potatoes in the steamer and bring the water to a boil over high heat. Sprinkle the potatoes with ½ teaspoon salt, then reduce the heat to medium-high. Steam for 9–10 minutes. The potatoes should be fork-tender but not mushy. Remove from the steamer. Let them cool completely. Once the potatoes are cool enough to handle and have dried, peel them and cut them into the same shapes as the salsify.

3. **Caramelizing the shallots:** Heat 1 tablespoon olive oil in a deep pan over high heat. Reduce to low heat and sauté the shallots in the oil for about 8 minutes, stirring frequently to prevent them from burning, until the color is evenly golden brown and the shallots are tender. Season with ¼ teaspoon salt. Transfer to a plate.

4. **Preparing the apple:** Peel, core, and cut the apple into pieces the same shape as the salsify. Drizzle with the lemon juice to prevent them

from browning. Set aside. Preheat the oven to 400°F.

5. **Cooking the filling:** In the same pan you cooked the shallots, melt a tablespoon of butter over medium-high heat. Add the potatoes. Reduce the heat to medium-low, so as not to burn the butter. Lightly cover the pan with a sheet of aluminum foil, and cook for 3 minutes. Flip the potatoes, and cook for another 3 minutes until lightly browned. Add the apples and salsify. Cook for an additional 2 minutes, then season with 1 teaspoon salt and ½ teaspoon pepper. Add 1 tablespoon each of curly parsley and the shallots. Set aside.

6. **Making Mornay sauce:** In the same pan, melt the rest of the butter over medium-low heat, making sure not to burn it. Add the thyme and marjoram, and cook for about 2 minutes until fragrant. Bring the heat back up to medium-high and add the flour. Keep stirring with a wooden spoon for approximately 2 minutes. The flour should absorb the butter and form a paste. Add the warm milk in 3 stages. Increase the heat to high while constantly stirring for 4–5 minutes. Reduce the heat to low. Add the Cheddar and 1 tablespoon of the Dubliner cheese. Season with the nutmeg and

mustard, if using. Salt and pepper to taste. Cook for another minute. Stir well. Let the sauce rest until it's time to assemble the dish.

7. **Assembly time:** Brush 6 individual ovenproof serving dishes with 1 tablespoon olive oil, then add the potato mixture. Spread a ladle of the Mornay sauce to cover the filling. Finish with a layer of Dubliner cheese. Bake in the oven for 10 minutes at 400°F, then broil for 2–3 minutes to get a nice golden top. Remove from the oven and let rest for at least 15 minutes. Serve warm. Garnish with the remaining parsley.

SALSIFY SUBSTITUTE   You can replace salsify with canned white asparagus or any other winter vegetables, such as rutabagas, parsnips, turnips, leeks, or kale; but you'll need to cook them first until tender, before you start the steps in this recipe.

Pommes de Terre Chamonix

YIELDS 8 SERVINGS

Pommes de terre Chamonix is the quintessential french-fried potato dish, but it's nothing like your typical french fry! Here, elegant and savory pâte à choux *dough is combined with cheesy mashed potatoes, piped into churro-like "cigars," then deep-fried until golden brown for a true gourmet treat.*

2 russet potatoes
¾ cup smoked Gouda cheese, finely grated
6 tablespoons unsalted butter
1 cup all-purpose flour

1 cup vegetable broth, warmed
⅛ teaspoon nutmeg, freshly grated
⅛ teaspoon salt
¼ teaspoon black pepper
6 eggs

2 teaspoons granulated sugar
1 quart canola oil, or more if needed

1. **Baking the potatoes:** Preheat the oven to 400°F. Scrub the potatoes, then pat them dry. Prick the skin all over with a small, sharp knife for faster cooking time. Bake for 1 hour and 15 minutes, until soft and tender. Once the potatoes are cool enough to handle, gently remove the skin with a paring knife and grate them using the largest holes of a box food grater. Add the Gouda cheese and mix well.

2. **Making the choux pastry dough:** In a saucepan, melt the butter over medium-low heat. When the butter is hot and golden, add the flour. Stir continuously with a wooden spoon for approximately 3 minutes. The flour should absorb the butter and form a paste. Add the warm vegetable broth in 3 stages, stirring to incorporate fully after each addition. Decrease the heat to low while constantly stirring for 2–3 minutes. Season with the nutmeg, salt, and pepper. Allow the mixture to cool; you could spread it on a flat surface to hasten the cooling time. Meanwhile, in a mixing bowl, beat the eggs with the sugar until the eggs are pale and thickened. Add the eggs to the flour mixture in 4 stages, and whisk until fully incorporated. Add the cheesy grated potatoes. Mix well. Transfer the dough to a pastry bag fitted with a ridged pastry tip. The cigars will be about 1" wide.

3. **Forming the pommes Chamonix:** Line two baking trays with silicone mats or sheets of parchment paper. Using the piping bag, create 4" long "cigar" shapes on the baking trays, making sure to space them at least 1" apart so they're easy to pick up. Using your finger, flatten both ends of the cigars by moistening them with water. Place in the freezer for about 15 minutes until firm.

Pommes de Terre Chamonix
continued

4. **Heating the oil:** Line a cooling rack with paper towels and stack it on top of a baking sheet for easy clean-up. In a large Dutch oven or deep fryer, heat the oil for 2 minutes over high heat. There should be at least 4" of oil in the fryer; add more if one quart of oil doesn't reach this level. The oil should be slightly bubbly, and a thermometer should register 345°F–360°F. Test the oil by dropping in a teaspoon of the batter; it should float, but not swell.

5. **Assembly time:** Place the pommes Chamonix in the hot oil in batches, making sure not to overcrowd. Deep-fry for 4–5 minutes until golden and crunchy, flipping each piece using a spider skimmer. Remove them to the draining rack. Repeat the same procedure for the rest of the pastries. Serve immediately.

VARIATIONS   Without cheese, this fried potato dish is called *pommes de terre Lorette*, and without the choux paste, they're *pommes duchesse*.

Broccoli and Cheddar Pierogies

YIELDS 4 SERVINGS

Pierogies are potato dumplings traditionally made with sautéed onions and sour cream. In this recipe, they are stuffed with broccoli, which gives them a unique green color, and flavored with a generous amount of cheddar cheese.

4 broccoli crowns
¼ cup regular white vinegar
2 tablespoons salt
2 pounds Yukon Gold potatoes
1¼ cups heavy cream, warmed
½ cup olive oil, as needed

2 yellow onions, 1 chopped, 1 thinly sliced
1 teaspoon dry mustard powder
½ cup sharp Cheddar cheese, freshly grated
1 teaspoon black pepper, freshly ground

1 whole egg
⅛ teaspoon red chili powder
1¼ cups all-purpose flour, as needed
1 cup sour cream, as needed
½ cup warm water
1 tablespoon unsalted butter

1. **Cooking the broccoli:** Wash the broccoli and separate the florets from the stems. Place the florets in a large bowl, cover them with water, and meanwhile, bring 1 quart cold water to a boil. Add the broccoli stems first, cook for 3 minutes in salted boiling water (1 teaspoon), then add the broccoli florets and cook for another 15 minutes. Drain and reserve a few florets for decoration later. Coarsely mash the broccoli. Adjust seasoning with more salt, to taste.

2. **Boiling the potatoes:** Cut the potatoes in half if they are too large (no more than 2" chunks). Wash the unpeeled potatoes and place them in a large pot. Add cold water until the potatoes are barely covered. Bring to a boil, add 1 teaspoon salt, and reduce the heat to medium. Boil the potatoes for 25–30 minutes, until tender. Remove from the pot. Drain the potatoes thoroughly and let them cool a little, but do not rinse. Once the

potatoes are dried and cool enough to handle, gently remove the skin using a paring knife. Cut into 1" cubes.

3. **Making the pierogi filling:** Warm the cream for a few minutes in a nonstick pot over low heat. In a separate large pan, heat 2 tablespoons oil over high heat. Add the chopped onion to the pan, and cook for 7–8 minutes, until golden. Reserve half the amount of the onions as garnish. Add the dry potatoes, and cook for 2–3 minutes. Turn off the heat. Using the back of a fork or a potato masher, coarsely mash the potatoes. Add the broccoli, cream, dry mustard, and cheese. Stir well. Season with salt and pepper to taste. Let cool to room temperature and chill in the refrigerator until ready to assemble.

4. **Making the pierogi dough:** In a bowl, lightly beat the egg with the red chili powder. Reserve

approximately 2 tablespoons flour. Place the remaining flour and ¼ teaspoon salt in a mixing bowl. Stir to combine. Form a well in the center of the bowl, then pour in the egg mixture and 2 tablespoons sour cream. Mix the dough using a pastry blender. Wet the dough with about ½ cup warm water until combined and a bit sticky, adding a little liquid at a time until you reach the right consistency. Add 2 tablespoons oil, then knead the dough until it becomes smooth. Transfer the dough to a lightly oiled bowl. Cover with a towel, place the bowl in a warm spot, and set aside until you're ready to assemble.

5. **Browning the onion:** In a large nonstick pan, heat some oil over high heat. Add the thinly sliced onion and cook for 8–10 minutes, until golden brown, stirring frequently to prevent them from burning. Set aside.

6. **Wrapping the pierogies:** Dust the work space with the reserved flour and roll the dough into a thin sheet, about ¹⁄₁₆" thick. Using a 3⅞" scalloped-edged circle cutter, form 12 equal disks from the dough sheet. Place about 2 tablespoons of the filling in the center of each disk, then fold the disk in half, into a half-moon shape. Seal the pierogi by forming small pleats along the edge and

pinching firmly. Repeat until all the ingredients are used.

7. **Boiling the pierogies:** Fill a large pot with 3 quarts of water and bring to a boil over high heat. Add the potato dumplings, bring back to a boil, then immediately lower the heat to a gentle boil. Cook for 3–4 minutes, until they float to the surface. Salt the water halfway through the cooking process (about 1 teaspoon), and gently stir occasionally so the pierogies don't stick to the bottom. Delicately lift the pierogies with a slotted spoon and let stand in a colander. Reserve about 1 cup of the dumpling water.

8. **Assembly time:** In the same pan used for the caramelized onions, heat 2 tablespoons oil over high heat. Place the pierogies into the pan and add the butter. Pan-fry them for 3–4 minutes until crisp and brown on both sides. Season with ¼ teaspoon each of salt and pepper. If the dumplings start sticking to the bottom, add some of the reserved water. Cover the pan and wait until the liquid is completely absorbed, then continue on. Add the reserved onion and broccoli florets. Transfer to a large serving platter. Garnish with a generous amount of sour cream in the middle. Serve immediately.

Chapter 4

crispy & crunchy

There's something special about crunchy potatoes. For many of us, the best and most classic potato preparations are those with crunch. Whether baked or fried, the textural contrast of the crispy shell and the soft, luscious interior is absolutely addictive. I've included some of the best classic roasted French potato recipes, from Lyonnaise Potatoes with Green Olives and Sun-Dried Tomatoes to Galettes de Pomme de Terre à l'Alsacienne.

While crunchy potatoes are wonderful when roasted to perfection with just a little salt and pepper, they present a perfect opportunity to layer flavors. Many of the recipes in this section are creative fusion dishes that use unexpected and even tropical ingredients to offer a vibrant counterpoint to the familiar crunch of the potato. From pesto to mango aioli, there are literally endless creative possibilities, and we explore some of the most delicious in this chapter!

Hasselback Potatoes with Sauce Verte

YIELDS 6 SERVINGS

Hasselback potatoes are a Swedish variation on roasted potatoes. The potatoes have a crispy outer skin with a delicious, soft inside. The cooking technique isn't different from common baked potatoes, except these potatoes are thinly sliced into an accordion shape. A blend of butter, extra-virgin olive oil, and garlic creates a crunchy outer crust that is perfectly seasoned. Once the potatoes are roasted, they fan out, but the bottom remains attached. The presentation may be fancy, but really, this dish isn't complicated at all.

3 cloves garlic, finely minced
½ teaspoon white pepper, freshly ground
2 teaspoons sea salt, to taste
6 tablespoons unsalted butter, softened to room temperature

6 tablespoons extra-virgin olive oil
12 medium-size new potatoes
1 teaspoon salt
1 bunch curly parsley
1 clove pickled garlic, finely minced

2 French gherkin pickles (*cornichons*), drained
2 tablespoons nonpareil capers, drained
1 teaspoon Dijon mustard
1 Meyer lemon, freshly squeezed

1. **Making the garlic-flavored butter:** Place 3 cloves garlic in a mortar and pestle. Add the pepper and 1 teaspoon sea salt. Blend the garlic into a thick paste and mix with the softened butter. Soften the mixture with 2 tablespoons extra-virgin olive oil.

2. **Parboiling the potatoes:** Wash the potatoes and place them whole and unpeeled into a large pot. Fill the pot with cold water until the potatoes are barely covered. Bring to a boil; add 1 teaspoon salt and reduce the heat to medium-high, then cook for 5–6 minutes. The potatoes should still be firm. Drain the potatoes thoroughly and let them cool a little. Once the potatoes are cool enough to handle, cut a thin slice to flatten one long side of the potato, creating a base so the potatoes remain stable while roasting in the oven.

3. **Preparing the potatoes:** Preheat oven to 425°F. Let the potato lie on its base and make a series of cuts toward the base, as though you were slicing the potato into ⅛" thick slices. Make sure you don't cut all the way through the base, so all the thin slices remain attached.

4. **Roasting the potatoes:** Brush a baking pan with olive oil. Place the potatoes on the greased baking pan. Bake for approximately 2 minutes to just dry out the potatoes. Once the potatoes have completely dried, remove the pan from the oven. Using a butter knife, spread a thin layer of the garlic butter mixture between each slice. Transfer

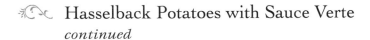

Hasselback Potatoes with Sauce Verte
continued

back into the hot oven and roast for approximately 45 minutes. When there's a nice brown crust and the potatoes open like a fan, they're ready! Sprinkle with additional sea salt, to taste.

5. **Making the sauce verte:** Sprinkle ½ teaspoon sea salt over the parsley and pickled garlic. Using a sharp knife, finely chop until the mixture becomes almost a purée, or use a food processor. The addition of the sea salt helps to get the right texture. Add the cornichons and capers. Coarsely chop. Transfer to a bowl; add the mustard, a squeeze of lemon juice, and ¼ cup olive oil. Stir well. Cover with a drizzle of olive oil until ready to serve.

6. **Assembly time:** When you're ready to serve, stir the sauce verte (at room temperature) and fill the potato accordions with it. Serve immediately.

Hasselback Potatoes with Sauce Verte

Parsley and Walnut Pesto Roasted Potatoes

YIELDS 10 SERVINGS

Pesto can be used to brighten up just about any type of dish. From pasta to salads, it adds color and intense flavor, with endless possibilities for creativity. You can create myriad variations by changing the oils, nuts, cheeses, and greens used. Experiment with your own flavor combinations and when combining with roasted potatoes, just make sure to always use a waxy potato. For this dish, you don't want the potatoes to turn mushy; cooking red-skinned potatoes won't affect their texture and shape.

½ cup extra-virgin olive oil
1 red onion, cut into thin wedges
6 tablespoons flat-leaf parsley (with stems), finely chopped
¼ cup walnuts, coarsely chopped

1 lemon, zested and juiced
2 teaspoons coarse sea salt
½ teaspoon black pepper, freshly ground
2 tablespoons goat ricotta cheese
1 teaspoon salt

5 pounds small red-skinned potatoes
6 tablespoons unsalted butter, softened to room temperature

1. **Making the pesto:** In a large, nonstick pan, heat 2 tablespoons olive oil over high heat. Add half the red onion and cook over low heat for about 5 minutes, stirring frequently to prevent the onion from burning, until the color is evenly golden brown. Transfer to a plate, leaving as much oil as possible in the pan. In a blender or a mini food processor, combine the parsley, the browned onions, chopped walnuts, ¼ cup olive oil, lemon zest, and lemon juice. Season with ½ teaspoon each of sea salt and black pepper. If your pesto is thicker than you like it to be, add a little water to thin it out somewhat. Transfer to a mixing bowl. Add the ricotta cheese and stir until the color is evenly green.

2. **Boiling the potatoes:** Wash the potatoes and cut them into 3" pieces. Place them in a large pot. Fill the pot with cold water until the potatoes are barely covered. Bring to a boil over high heat, add salt, reduce the heat to medium-high, and cook for 20–25 minutes. The potatoes should be fork-tender but still firm. Remove from the pot. Drain the potatoes thoroughly and let them cool a little. Once the potatoes are cool enough to handle and have dried, toss them to coat with the pesto.

3. **Roasting the potatoes:** Preheat the oven to 425°F. Place the potatoes and remaining raw red onion wedges into a greased baking dish. Drizzle with 2 tablespoons olive oil. Season with sea salt and pepper. Roast for 30–35 minutes. Serve warm.

Pommes de Terre Rôties au Four

My family has been on a bit of a quest for the perfect roasted potatoes. After many attempts to cook a potato that is crunchy on the outside, soft on the inside, and perfectly seasoned throughout, I've come up with a tried and true method for consistently great crunchy potatoes. With the right combination of herbs, this dish can go from being an everyday kitchen table staple to an elegant, eye-catching addition to any dinner party.

1 sprig fresh rosemary, finely chopped	2 teaspoons coarse sea salt	2 tablespoons extra-virgin olive oil
3 sprigs fresh thyme, finely chopped	½ teaspoon black pepper, freshly cracked	6 pounds Yukon Gold potatoes, peeled
3 sprigs fresh marjoram, finely chopped	6 tablespoons unsalted butter, softened to room temperature	1 tablespoon salt
1 tablespoon garlic powder		

1. **Making the herb-flavored butter:** Place the fresh herbs, garlic powder, sea salt, and pepper in a mini prep food processor or regular food processor. Using the fastest speed, grind the spices into a fine powder, then add the butter. Pulse the mixture until it's creamy. If it's too thick and doesn't look spreadable, add a tablespoon of olive oil. Set aside.

2. **Boiling the potatoes:** Wash the potatoes and cut them into 3" pieces. Depending on the size of the potatoes, you can cut them smaller, but it's important that they are all a uniform size. Place them in a large pot and fill it with cold water until the potatoes are barely covered. Bring to a boil over high heat; add salt and reduce the heat to medium-high, cooking for 20–25 minutes. The potatoes should be fork-tender but still firm. Remove from the pot. Drain the potatoes

thoroughly and let them cool a little. Once the potatoes are cool enough to handle and have dried, gather them in a mixing bowl. Spread the flavored butter mixture and toss well to coat.

3. **Roasting the potatoes:** Preheat the oven to 425°F. Place the potatoes in an oiled baking dish. Roast for 30–35 minutes. When there's a nice golden brown crust, the potatoes are ready. Serve warm.

PROPERLY SEASONING ROASTED POTATOES

The trick to proper seasoning in this particular recipe is to overseason! When you prepare the herb butter mix, you'll want to make it slightly more salty than you might otherwise think, because it will help to compensate for the relative lack of seasoning at the center of each potato.

Lyonnaise Potatoes with Green Olives and Sun-Dried Tomatoes

YIELDS 8 SERVINGS

Lyonnaise potatoes originated in the city of Lyon, which is famous as a main center of French gastronomy. Generally, pommes de terre lyonnaises is a crisp yet tender potato dish; sliced caramelized onions, combined with olives and sun-dried tomatoes, are added to this recipe for color and a mild contrast of flavor. These potatoes are the perfect accompaniment to any meat dish.

3 pounds Yukon Gold potatoes
1 tablespoon kosher salt (or regular salt)
3 tablespoons olive oil
2 yellow onions, sliced
1 shallot, sliced

4 cloves garlic, finely minced
2 tablespoons unsalted butter, diced
1 teaspoon white pepper, freshly ground
8 green Greek olives, pitted and coarsely chopped

3 tablespoons sun-dried tomatoes in olive oil, coarsely chopped
2 tablespoons curly parsley, chopped

1. **Parboiling the potatoes:** Wash the potatoes, and place them whole and unpeeled in a large pot. Fill the pot with cold water until the potatoes are barely covered. Bring to a boil over high heat; add 1 teaspoon salt and reduce the heat to medium-high, cooking for about 8 minutes. The potatoes should still be firm. Drain the potatoes thoroughly and let them cool a little. Once the potatoes are cool enough to handle, remove the skin. Cut them into ½" slices.

2. **Caramelizing the onions and shallot:** Heat the olive oil in a large, heavy-bottomed skillet over low heat. Sauté the onions and shallot in the oil over low heat for 8–10 minutes, stirring frequently to prevent them from burning, until the color is evenly golden brown and the onions are tender. Season with 1 teaspoon salt. Add the garlic and cook for 2 minutes, until slightly golden. Leaving as much oil as possible in the skillet, transfer the vegetables to a platter. Set aside.

3. **Browning the potatoes:** Preheat the oven to 400°F. Divide the sliced potatoes into 4 batches. In the same skillet that you cooked the onion, melt 2 tablespoons butter over medium heat. Add the first batch of potatoes, being sure not to over-crowd the skillet. Lightly cover the pan with a sheet of aluminum foil. Cook for 5–6 minutes. Using a silicone spatula, carefully flip the potatoes, so they remain crispy and intact. Cook the other side for another 3–4 minutes, until nicely browned. Season with salt and white pepper and

set aside the first batch of potatoes. Repeat with
the rest of the batches until all the potatoes are
browned on both sides. Place the potatoes in a
greased baking dish and finish cooking them in
the oven for 15 minutes. Check for doneness;
they should be crispy on the outside and soft on
the inside. Adjust seasoning to taste.

4. **Assembly time:** Sprinkle the caramelized
onions, olives, and sun-dried tomatoes over the
potatoes. Let the potatoes stand in the oven at
200°F to keep warm until ready to serve. Sprinkle
with curly parsley and serve hot.

Lyonnaise Potatoes with Green
Olives and Sun-Dried Tomatoes

Crispy Potato Wedges

YIELDS 10 SERVINGS

In France, these crispy, breaded potato wedges are actually called country potatoes. Just as American dishes are given French-sounding names to make them sound more appealing, in France, American dishes are perpetually in vogue. On my last trip to France, I noticed that among the locals, American hot dogs were outselling French baguette sandwiches and savory tarts in the bakeries! Quelle horreur! *No matter what name you ascribe to this dish, though, it will still look and taste delicious.*

1 slice 1-day-old stale wheat bread (or white bread), diced
1 teaspoon dried basil
1 teaspoon dried parsley flakes
1 teaspoon ground coriander

1 teaspoon cayenne pepper
1 teaspoon onion powder
1½ teaspoons garlic powder
2 teaspoons coarse sea salt
½ teaspoon black pepper, freshly ground

4 russet potatoes, peeled
1 tablespoon sour cream
2 tablespoons extra-virgin olive oil
3 tablespoons canola oil

1. **Making the bread crumbs:** Put the diced bread into a food processor, or a mini food processor, and pulse several times into fine powder. Add the seasoning ingredients and 2 teaspoons salt and ½ teaspoon pepper. Stir and set aside.

2. **Preparing the potatoes:** Preheat the oven to 375°F. Cut the potatoes into small, thick wedges. Place them in a sealable container. Add the sour cream and 1 tablespoon olive oil. Cover with a lid and shake until well coated with sour cream and oil. Add the seasoned bread crumbs and repeat the same procedure until well combined.

3. **Assembly time:** Place the potatoes onto an oiled baking pan. Drizzle with one more tablespoon olive oil. Toss well. Bake for 50–60 minutes until golden brown. Serve warm.

Oven Sweet Potato Fries with Pineapple-Mango Aioli

YIELDS 8 SERVINGS

The real key to successfully making this dish is to have a flavorful condiment to pair it with. I have served them with a chutney-style flavored mayonnaise for a spicy kick. A sweet mango chutney would also be an excellent choice.

3 pounds sweet potatoes
¾ cup olive oil, as needed
1 teaspoon smoked paprika
¼ teaspoon freshly ground cinnamon
1¼ teaspoons kosher salt
1 cardamom pod

⅛ teaspoon cumin seeds
1 teaspoon freshly grated ginger
1 teaspoon freshly grated garlic
¼ cup mango purée, store-bought
⅛ teaspoon cayenne pepper
1 tablespoon dark floral honey

2 tablespoons canned crushed pineapple
1 egg yolk, at room temperature
1 teaspoon Dijon mustard, at room temperature

1. **Baking the sweet potatoes:** Preheat the oven to 425°F. Peel and cut the sweet potatoes into ½"–1" sticks. Place them in a sealable bag and drizzle with 2 tablespoons olive oil. Close the bag and shake until well coated with oil. Add the paprika, cinnamon, and 1 teaspoon salt. Place the potatoes onto an oiled baking pan. Drizzle with ¼ cup olive oil and toss well. Bake for 50–60 minutes, until golden. Gently toss the potatoes and rotate the pan halfway through the baking process.

2. **Preparing the cardamom:** Remove the seeds from the pod shell and, in a mortar and pestle, grind the seeds. Crush them and gather the cardamom powder.

3. **Making the mango chutney:** In a deep saucepan, heat 1 tablespoon olive oil over high heat. Add the cumin seeds. Once the seeds start popping in the hot oil, add the ginger, garlic, ground cardamom, mango, and cayenne powder. Cook over high heat for 3 minutes, until the mixture thickens. Add the honey and season with ¼ teaspoon salt. Reduce the heat to a gentle simmer, then stir in the crushed pineapple. Bring to a rolling boil, then immediately turn off the heat. Strain the mango mixture through a sieve. Set aside.

4. **Making the aioli:** In a bowl, whisk the egg yolk, then add the Dijon mustard. Stirring continuously and very slowly, add ½ cup oil a little at a time until fully combined. Whisk until emulsified.

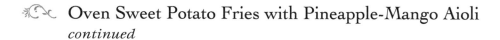
Add 2 tablespoons mango chutney mixture. Stir until the color is uniform. Season with salt and pepper.

5. **Assembly time:** Serve the potatoes warm with aioli on the side.

THE PERFECT TEXTURE FOR THE AIOLI If you find that your aioli is unpleasantly thick, you can add 1–2 tablespoons boiling water. If it's too watery, add the 2 extra tablespoons oil. If you've tried both solutions and the aioli isn't set, whisk in another egg yolk with a little juice from the crushed pineapple. Let sit at room temperature until you're ready to serve.

Galettes de Pomme de Terre à l'Alsacienne

YIELDS 6 SERVINGS

For a long time, this old Alsatian dish was difficult to find on restaurant menus in France. But what's old is new, as the saying goes, and now it's enjoying a bit of a resurgence. These rustic galettes are a mix of potatoes, shallots, leeks, a little flour, eggs, and parsley. They go great with a French-cut rack of lamb accompanied with warm compote de pommes (apple sauce) and braised red cabbage.

2 pounds russet potatoes	2 eggs	1½ teaspoons kosher salt
1 lemon, freshly squeezed	⅛ teaspoon cayenne pepper (optional)	½ teaspoon black pepper, freshly ground
2 tablespoons curly parsley, chopped	3 tablespoons all-purpose flour	1 cup canola oil, as needed
4 shallots, chopped	¼ teaspoon nutmeg, freshly grated	
1 3" piece leek (white part only), chopped	¼ teaspoon baking powder	

1. **Preparing the potatoes:** Wash and peel the potatoes. Shred ⅔ of them and place them in a large mixing bowl. Add the lemon juice and cover with cold water. Let sit for 5–10 minutes. Drain the potatoes using a fine mesh colander and discard the liquid. Place all the shredded potatoes in a cheesecloth and remove as much excess water as possible, then pat dry with paper towels. Place aside in a large bowl. Coarsely chop the remaining ⅓ of the potatoes. Place them into the bowl of a food processor. Add the parsley, shallots, and leek. Pulse into a smooth raw purée. Add the mixture to the shredded potatoes.

2. **Making the batter:** In a mixing bowl, beat the eggs with the cayenne pepper for 2–3 minutes, until slightly thickened. Add the nutmeg and baking powder. Add the eggs to the potato mix. Season with 1 teaspoon salt and ½ teaspoon pepper. Stir well.

3. **Frying the galettes:** In a large Dutch oven or regular deep fryer, heat the oil for 2–3 minutes over high heat. You should have at least 1" of oil in the pot. Wait until the oil is slightly bubbly over high heat. Grease disposable food-safe gloves with oil and use your hands to form small flattened patties. Lower the heat to medium-high, then place the patties in the oil in batches, making sure the galettes don't touch each other. Lower the heat to medium-low for even cooking and to prevent them from browning too fast. Fry for 5–8 minutes per batch until golden. Flip each piece using a spider skimmer and cook for

about 3 minutes, until crispy on both sides. Delicately lift each fritter, draining as much oil as possible, and transfer them onto a cooling rack. Season with salt. Continue the procedure with the remaining galettes. Reset the heat each time so the galettes don't burn.

4. **Assembly time:** Once the galettes are all cooked, maintain their temperature at 170°F in the oven to keep the dish warm until you're ready to serve.

Khoai Lan Chiên Tôm

YIELDS 24 APPETIZERS

In Vietnam, this sweet potato and shrimp dish is served on many street corners. Three matchsticks of sweet potato and a whole shrimp adhered to them are dipped in a tempura batter, and then the whole thing is deep fried. Unlike many street foods that taste quite a bit better than they look, these fried treats are elegant and sensual, and would be at home on any Asian-inspired dinner menu.

2 cups all-purpose flour	3½ teaspoons salt	2 cloves garlic, finely minced
½ cup cornstarch	2⅔ – 3 cups seltzer water	3 sweet potatoes
½ teaspoon turmeric	8 ounces crushed ice (1½ cups)	1 quart peanut oil (or regular vegetable oil), for deep frying, as needed
1 tablespoon baking powder	¼ cup rice flour	
1 teaspoon sugar	1 teaspoon black pepper, freshly ground	
1 teaspoon red chili powder	2 pounds large shrimp	

1. **Making the tempura flour:** Combine the all-purpose flour, cornstarch, turmeric, baking powder, ¼ teaspoon sugar, ½ teaspoon red chili powder, and 2 teaspoons salt. Sift together.

2. **Making the tempura batter:** Divide the seltzer water into 2 measuring cups: one with 2⅓ cups and another with ⅓ cup. Add the 2⅓ cups seltzer water and the crushed ice to the tempura flour until incorporated. Do not overmix; it's okay if the batter is still lumpy. In another bowl, dissolve the rice flour into ⅓ cup seltzer water. Combine the two mixtures and stir them together. Once more, do not over-mix, or you'll be left with a less airy result. The consistency of the tempura batter should be similar to pancake batter. If the batter is too thick, add the remaining seltzer water. Allow to rest for an hour in the refrigerator.

3. **Preparing the shrimp:** In a bowl, combine 1½ teaspoons salt, ¾ teaspoon sugar, ½ teaspoon red chili powder, and pepper. If you happen to be using frozen shrimp, it's not necessary to thaw them. Remove and discard the head of the shrimp if it's still attached. Carefully shell and devein the shrimp, leaving the tail on, if possible. Rinse the shrimp under cold running water and pat dry using a paper towel. Spread the shrimp on a large tray, then generously coat the shrimp with the garlic. Sprinkle the shrimp with ½ teaspoon red chili powder, add 2 teaspoons oil, and coat well. Wrap the tray in plastic and let the shrimp marinate for 15–20 minutes in the refrigerator.

4. **Preparing the sweet potatoes:** Peel and cut the sweet potatoes into 1"–1½" inch matchsticks.

5. **Deep frying:** Layer a cooling rack lined with paper towels on top of a baking sheet. Meanwhile, in a large Dutch oven or regular deep fryer, heat at least 2" of oil for 2 minutes over high heat until slightly bubbly, approximately 350°F–375°F. Add 2 teaspoons oil to the tempura batter. Stir well. Test the oil by dropping a teaspoon of tempura batter into the hot oil. It should float but not swell. Using a spatula, gather 3 sweet potato matchsticks. Dip a shrimp into the tempura batter to coat completely. Allow the excess batter to drip back into the tempura batter bowl. Place a shrimp on top of the 3 matchsticks. Drizzle an additional teaspoon tempura batter over the shrimp to ensure that it adheres well to the sweet potatoes, then place the shrimp and potato combination in the hot oil. Fry in batches, making sure the shrimp fritters don't touch each other. Lower the heat to medium. Deep-fry for approximately 3 minutes per batch. The fritters will start to pop and increase in volume. Flip each piece using a spider skimmer and cook for about a minute until golden on all sides.

6. **Assembly time:** Remove each fritter, draining as much oil as possible and transfer them to the cooling rack. Continue the procedure with the remaining shrimp. Serve immediately. You can eat the shrimp fritters simply as is or wrapped in lettuce filled with Thai basil, cilantro, and Vietnamese mint.

Pommes Parisiennes

YIELDS 4 SERVINGS

Pommes Parisiennes are named after a kitchen utensil, a Parisienne scoop. It looks similar to a melon baller, except it's slightly larger. The potato balls are formed from large, raw, floury potatoes, then parboiled and pan-fried until golden. They're a delicious and delicately sized potato treat that's a perfect fit for any party!

3 pounds Yukon Gold potatoes
1 tablespoon kosher salt (or regular salt), as needed
3 tablespoons olive oil

2 tablespoons unsalted butter
1 teaspoon white pepper, freshly ground

1. **Forming the potato balls:** Peel the potatoes. Using a Parisienne scoop, form as many 1½"-diameter balls as possible. Place them in a large bowl. Reserve the remaining potato for making soup or mashed potatoes. Cover the potato balls with ice water. Let sit for at least 2 hours, then drain the potatoes.

2. **Parboiling the potatoes:** Place the potatoes in a large pot and fill it with cold water until the potatoes are barely covered. Bring to a boil over high heat and reduce the heat to medium-high, cooking the potatoes for 3–4 minutes. Drain the potatoes.

3. **Assembly time:** Preheat the oven to 200°F. In a large, heavy-bottomed skillet, heat the oil over high heat. Add the potatoes. Sprinkle with ½ teaspoon salt and toss well. Reduce the heat to medium-low. Cook for up to 30 minutes until golden. Frequently turn so all sides are nicely browned. At the end of cooking time, add the butter and season with 2 teaspoons salt and 1 teaspoon pepper. Check for doneness of the potatoes. They should be crispy on the outside and soft on the inside. Adjust seasoning to taste. Let the potatoes stand in the oven at 200°F until ready to serve.

POMMES NOISETTE AND POMMES PARISIENNES

Noisette in French means hazelnut. If you form the potato balls with a melon baller, and cook them as you would Parisian potatoes, the dish is called *pommes noisette*.

Pommes Parisiennes

Moules Frites

YIELDS 4 SERVINGS

Moules frites—popular in both Belgium and France—is an irresistible combination of wine-flavored steamed mussels accompanied with crispy french fries. The twist here is that the fries are seasoned with a citrus zest-flavored sea salt. Pair the mussels and fries with a blonde beer—a popular European pale beer—and you'll have an unforgettable meal.

1 tablespoon sea salt, to taste

2 teaspoons *fines herbes*

1 lemon, zested

1 teaspoon fresh ginger, very finely diced

⅛ teaspoon nutmeg, freshly grated

2 tablespoons olive oil

2 shallots, finely chopped

1 clove garlic, finely minced

1 star anise, lightly crushed

2 tablespoons garlic chives, snipped into 1" pieces

2 tablespoons celery, peeled and chopped

2 bay leaves

1 tablespoon black peppercorns

3 pounds mussels, cleaned and de-bearded

1½ cups dry white wine

2 teaspoons salt

1½ pounds Yukon Gold potatoes

1 quart canola oil, as needed

1. **Making the ginger citrus sea salt:** In a mortar and pestle, combine the sea salt, *fines herbes*, lemon zest, ginger, and nutmeg. Coarsely grind until the salt is moist and fragrant.

2. **Steaming the mussels:** In a large stock pot, heat the olive oil over high heat. Add the shallots and garlic. Cook for 4–5 minutes until golden. Add the star anise, chives, celery, bay leaves, black peppercorns, and lemon (cut into ½" slices). Stir well. Add the mussels. Cover with the white wine and 2 cups water. Bring to a boil over high heat, and stir well. Cook for 3–5 minutes, then cover with a lid and turn off the heat. Let stand for 5 minutes. Season with 1 teaspoon salt. The mussels should open; discard any that do not (they were not fresh). Keep the pot covered until the fries are ready.

3. **Frying the potatoes:** Trim about ½" from both ends of the unpeeled potatoes. Peel the potatoes, and cut them into ½" thick and 4" long sticks. Place them in a large bowl; cover them with ice water, and let sit for at least 15 minutes. Drain the potatoes and discard the liquid, removing as much excess water as possible. Pat dry using paper towels. Heat the canola oil in a deep-fryer, until a thermometer registers between 290°F and 310°F. In batches, place the potatoes into the fryer, being careful not to overcrowd, and cook for 6–7 minutes. The fries will still be pale at this point. Transfer to a platter lined with paper towels. Store in the refrigerator until all of

the potatoes have gone through this initial fry. You can hold the fries in the refrigerator until you're ready to serve them. When you're almost ready to serve, raise the temperature of the oil in the deep-fryer to 360°F–400°F. In batches, return the fries to the deep fryer, and cook for 3–4 minutes until golden and crispy. Delicately lift them, draining as much oil as possible, and transfer them to cooling racks lined with paper towels. Immediately season with a little salt (approximately 1 teaspoon regular salt total; the fries are seasoned twice). Continue with the remaining potatoes. In between batches of fries, you should filter the oil, and you should change the oil every fifth batch or so. When the fries are ready, season a second time with the ginger citrus sea salt. Toss well.

4. **Assembly time:** Serve the mussels in deep individual serving dishes with the french fries on the side. Sprinkle both the mussels and fries with a little more ginger citrus sea salt.

Mimolette Fines Herbes Pommes Pont-Neuf

YIELDS 4 SERVINGS

Pommes Pont-Neuf might sound impressive, but in this case, it simply means fries that are a bit larger in size than average french fries. This dish is the upscale equivalent of cheesy fries, with the nutty flavor and bright orange color of Mimolette cheese making the dish familiar and fresh at the same time. Serve them at your next tea party and you'll be guaranteed to amaze your guests.

1½ pounds russet potatoes
1 quart canola oil, as needed
2 teaspoons salt
½ teaspoon black pepper, freshly cracked

2 tablespoons coarse sea salt
¾ cup extra-aged Mimolette cheese, freshly grated

2 teaspoons French tarragon, finely chopped
2 teaspoons curly parsley, finely chopped

1. **Preparing the potatoes:** Trim both ends of the potatoes. Peel and cut the potatoes into ¾" thick and 5" long strips. Place in a large bowl and cover with ice water. Let sit for at least 15 minutes. Drain the potatoes and discard the liquid, removing as much excess water as possible. Pat dry using paper towels.

2. **Frying the potatoes:** Heat the oil in a deep-fryer, until a thermometer registers between 290°F and 310°F. Fry the potatoes in batches, being careful not to overcrowd the pot, and cook for 6–7 minutes. The fries will be still pale at this point. Do not overcook; the fries will finish frying in the second oil bath. Transfer to a platter lined with paper towels. Store in the refrigerator until you're almost ready to serve. When it's time to complete the dish, raise the temperature of the oil in the deep-fryer to 360°F–400°F. In batches, return the fries to the deep fryer and cook for 3–4 minutes until golden and crispy. Delicately lift the fries, draining as much oil as possible, and transfer them to cooling racks lined with paper towels. Immediately season with 1 teaspoon regular salt and ½ teaspoon pepper. Continue with the remaining potatoes. As you fry, you should filter the oil between batches, and change it out completely every fifth batch or so. Once all of the fries are ready, season a second time with the sea salt. Toss well.

3. **Baking the fries:** Preheat the oven to 425°F. Transfer all the fries to a nonstick baking pan. Drizzle with 1 tablespoon canola oil. Bake for 2–3 minutes. Open the oven, sprinkle the fries with the Mimolette cheese, and continue to bake for 6 more minutes. Gently toss them; rotate the pan halfway through the baking process.

Mimolette Fines Herbes Pommes Pont-Neuf
continued

4. **Assembly time:** Garnish with tarragon and parsley. Toss well, and serve hot!

MIMOLETTE CHEESE   Mimolette is a French cheese, made with cow's milk. When extra-aged (*extra-vieille*), it looks similar to a cantaloupe and has a pleasant nutty flavor. You could substitute Dutch Edam cheese or Parmesan for the Mimolette.

Chapter 5

creamy

Creamy mashed potatoes are like the perfect cocktail dress: simple and seductive. It's somewhat ironic, considering that if one were to eat mashed potatoes on a regular basis, it would be pretty difficult to fit into that little black dress!

Like most of the simple things in life, there is an art to making delicious mashed potatoes. They should be creamy but not soupy, firm but not lumpy, and always richly flavored. Once the basics are mastered, the opportunities for creativity are endless. Within this chapter, you'll find creamy mashed potatoes paired with dynamic, exciting flavors like those in the Brie Cheese and Roasted-Garlic Mashed Potatoes dish; you'll also find them paired with classic recipes in new and surprising ways, as in the Veal Hachis Parmentier (Shepherd's Pie). While many of the recipes in the section are fully self-contained meals, these dishes also pair exceptionally well with meat, so you have the flexibility to serve them when and how you want. Who says elegant can't be sensible?

Pomme Purée aux Olives

YIELDS 6 SERVINGS

The idea for making olive-flavored mashed potatoes came from strolling through Parisian open-air markets. Most of them carry the most delicious varieties of olives that are not overly salty. Much like a painting hanging in the Louvre or Musée d'Orsay, mashed potatoes act as a canvas upon which the color and flavor of the olives can shine.

10 ounces whole green olives, to taste (see sidebar)

2 pounds Yukon Gold potatoes

2¼ teaspoons salt, to taste

1½ cups cream, to taste

½ cup extra-virgin olive oil, to taste

½ teaspoon nutmeg, freshly grated

½ teaspoon white pepper, freshly ground

1 tablespoon curly parsley leaves, chopped

1. **Preparing the olives:** Pit and coarsely chop the olives, and set them aside.

2. **Boiling the potatoes:** Cut the potatoes in half. Wash the potatoes and place them unpeeled in a large pot. Add cold water until the potatoes are barely covered. Bring to a boil over high heat, add 1 teaspoon salt, and reduce the heat to medium-high. As soon as the water reaches a boil, cook for 25–30 minutes. Test, using a fork; the potatoes should be tender. Remove from the pot. Drain the potatoes thoroughly and let them cool a little, but do not rinse. Once the potatoes are cool enough to handle and have drained completely, gently remove the skin using a paring knife. Cut them into large cubes.

3. **Making the mashed potatoes:** In a separate saucepan, warm the cream for a few minutes over low heat. Return the potatoes to a nonstick pot and heat them over low heat for a few minutes to ensure they are as dry as possible. Add 2 tablespoons oil, then cook the potatoes for another 2–3 minutes. Turn off the heat. Using the back of a fork or a potato masher, coarsely mash the potatoes. Add the remaining olive oil, nutmeg, the warm cream, white pepper, and 1 teaspoon parsley if using. Stir well, using a wooden spoon. Add more cream until mixture reaches desired consistency. Add the chopped green olives and mix well. Finish with parsley.

SELECTING OLIVES

I use Lucques olives, which come from the Hérault region (le Languedoc), in the south of France. They're picked from September until mid-October and are delicious bright green olives that are large, meaty, and slightly sweet with a nutty taste. Lucques olives have an aroma of watercress with a hint of berries, and the flesh is quite firm. They're ideal paired with poultry and potato dishes.

Brie Cheese and Roasted-Garlic Mashed Potatoes

YIELDS 10 SERVINGS

The secret to incredibly fluffy mashed potatoes is to use a combination of heavy cream, crème fraîche, and butter. There are a lot of rich ingredients going on in this mashed potato recipe, but once you try it, you'll never want to go back. For added flavor, try roasting a head of garlic and squeezing the contents into the dish—it's impossible to resist.

1 head fresh garlic	½ teaspoon kosher salt	4 tablespoons butter
1 tablespoon olive oil	3½ pounds russet potatoes	1 8-ounce Brie cheese wheel, rind removed and coarsely chopped
1 tablespoon lemon juice, freshly squeezed	3 teaspoons salt	1 teaspoon white pepper, freshly ground
1 teaspoon lemon thyme, finely chopped	1 cup crème fraîche	1 teaspoon lemon zest, freshly grated
	¾ cup heavy cream, as needed	

1. **Roasting the garlic:** Preheat the oven to 400°F. Cut the top off the head of garlic, exposing the cloves. Drizzle with the olive oil and lemon juice. Sprinkle with the thyme and the kosher salt. Wrap in aluminum foil; roast for 1 hour. Allow to cool, then squeeze out the garlic cloves and set aside.

2. **Boiling the potatoes:** Peel the potatoes, cut them into 2" chunks, and place them in a large pot. Fill it with cold water until the potatoes are barely covered. Bring to a boil over high heat, add 1 teaspoon salt, and reduce the heat to medium-high. Boil gently for 20–25 minutes. The potatoes should be fork-tender. Remove from the pot and drain; allow the potatoes to cool a little.

3. **Assembly time:** Warm the crème fraîche and the heavy cream in two separate saucepans over low heat.

Preheat the oven to 350°F. Once the potatoes are cool enough to handle and have drained thoroughly, return them to their pot over low heat for a few minutes to evaporate any remaining liquid. Turn off the heat. Using a potato masher or a potato ricer, mash the potatoes. Add the butter, the puréed roasted garlic, Brie cheese, white pepper, and lemon zest. Stir well, using a wooden spoon. Add the warm crème fraîche, then add the heavy cream until you reach the desired consistency. Transfer to a casserole dish and bake for 30 minutes until a golden crust is formed. Serve hot.

MASHING THE POTATOES A big no-no is to mash the potatoes in a food processor or a blender; the best way to mash them is to use a food mill, a potato masher, or a potato ricer. You can also manually mash the potatoes using food service disposable gloves. And most important, make sure you don't overwork the mashed potatoes.

Veal Hachis Parmentier (Shepherd's Pie)

YIELDS 10 SERVINGS

Scottish folks may claim shepherd's pie as their own invention, but it's an unambiguously French version of the dish that was created for Louis XVI by apothecary proprietor Antoine Parmentier. Louis XVI was so taken with the dish that it became a royal staple, and he even took to wearing a potato flower on his lapel. This version is made with luxurious ground veal, befitting the decadence of this French king and his cake-eating queen.

- 3 tablespoons olive oil
- 1 yellow onion, finely chopped
- 2 cloves garlic, finely minced
- 1 teaspoon dried mustard
- ½ teaspoon paprika
- 1 sprig fresh thyme, chopped
- ⅛ teaspoon cayenne powder

- 1 14-ounce can chopped fire-roasted tomatoes
- 1 pound ground veal
- 2 tablespoons Greek-style plain yogurt
- 1 4.5-ounce tube tomato paste
- ½–1 cup beef stock, as needed
- 1½ teaspoons salt

- ½ teaspoon black pepper, freshly ground
- 1½ pounds russet potatoes
- ½ cup heavy cream (or whole milk)
- ¼ cup milk, as needed
- 10 tablespoons unsalted butter
- ½ cup Dubliner cheese, shaved

1. **Cooking the meat:** Preheat the oven to 375°F. Heat 2 tablespoons olive oil in a large, deep nonstick pan over medium heat. Add the onion and cook for 8 minutes until golden brown. Increase the heat to medium-high and add the garlic. Cook for about 2 minutes until fragrant. Add the dry mustard, paprika, sprig fresh thyme, and cayenne powder. Decrease the heat medium-low and add the tomatoes. Simmer for about 10 minutes until a little of the liquid evaporates and the mixture becomes thicker. Bring the heat back to high and add the ground meat. Separate the veal as it cooks in the pan, and cook until the meat changes color, then add the yogurt. Add the tomato paste and ½ cup beef stock, stirring the meat occasionally. Wait for the mixture to reach a full boil, then immediately turn the heat down to a simmer.

Season with salt and ¼ teaspoon pepper. Cover with a lid and cook for 20–25 minutes. Check the liquid, and periodically add ¼–½ cup beef stock if all the previous liquid is absorbed. Gently stir the mixture. Check seasoning and adjust to taste. Remove from heat and set aside.

2. **Boiling the potatoes:** Peel the potatoes, cut them into 2" chunks, and place them in a large pot. Fill it with cold water until the potatoes are barely covered. Bring to a boil over high heat, add 1 teaspoon salt, and reduce the heat to medium-high. Cook for 20–25 minutes. The potatoes should be fork-tender. Remove from the pot and drain; allow the potatoes to cool a little.

3. **Making the mashed potatoes:** Combine the heavy cream and milk, and warm in a saucepan over low heat. Once the potatoes are cool enough to handle and have drained thoroughly, return them to their pot over low heat for a few moments to be sure they're completely dried. Turn off the heat. Using a potato ricer, mash the potatoes. Add the butter, stirring vigorously. Add the warm cream and milk until you reach a slightly thinner consistency. For a silky-smooth consistency, pass the mashed potatoes through a coarse-mesh sieve, using a silicone scraper to push them through.

4. **Assembly time:** Brush a shallow 2-quart casserole dish with 1 tablespoon olive oil. Transfer the reserved onion to the casserole dish. Spread a layer of the ground veal and tomatoes. Cover with mashed potatoes. Finish by sprinkling with Dubliner cheese. Bake in the oven for 15 minutes until a golden crust is formed. At the end of the cooking time, if the potatoes are not golden brown enough, change your oven setting to broil for 2–3 minutes. Remove from the oven and let cool for at least 15 minutes. Serve warm.

Veal Hachis Parmentier (Shepherd's Pie)

Pesto Buttermilk Mashed Potatoes

YIELDS 8 SERVINGS

You may not believe it, but buttermilk mashed potatoes are just as fluffy as regular mashed potatoes made with heavy cream. The only difference is a pleasant tangy taste from the buttermilk. Here, homemade pistachio-basil pesto enhances the flavor of the mashed potatoes. There is nothing subtle about this dish; it's absolutely bursting with color and flavor.

½ bunch curly parsley
½ bunch sweet basil
1 clove pickled garlic
¼ cup pistachios, lightly toasted
¼ cup pecorino cheese

½ lemon, zested and freshly squeezed
¼ cup extra-virgin olive oil
2 teaspoons sea salt (or regular salt)
¾ teaspoon white pepper, freshly ground

3 pounds russet potatoes (about 5 large)
⅓ cup milk, at room temperature
6 tablespoons butter, diced
1 cup buttermilk, at room temperature

1. **Making the pistachio-basil pesto:** Blanch the parsley and basil for ten seconds in boiling water, then plunge into an ice bath to stop the cooking. Drain them, pat dry on a paper towel, and roughly chop. In a mini food processor or mini blender, combine the parsley and basil, pickled garlic, pistachios, Pecorino cheese, lemon juice, and lemon zest. Pulse and slowly add the olive oil until it becomes a smooth paste. If the pesto seems thicker than you would like, thin it out with a few teaspoons of water. Season with sea salt and pepper, to taste.

2. **Boiling the potatoes:** Peel the potatoes, cut them into 2" chunks and place them in a large pot. Fill it with cold water until the potatoes are barely covered. Bring to a boil over high heat, add 1 teaspoon salt, and reduce the heat to medium-high. Cook for 20–25 minutes. The potatoes should be fork-tender. Drain the potatoes thoroughly and let them cool; don't rinse them.

3. **Assembly time:** Once the potatoes are cool enough to handle, return them to the pot for 2–3 minutes over low heat, to ensure there is as little liquid remaining as possible. Turn off the heat. Using a potato masher or a potato ricer, mash the potatoes. Add the milk, butter, and 3 tablespoons pesto. Stir well. Add the buttermilk until you reach the desired consistency. Season with 1 teaspoon salt and ½ teaspoon white pepper. Top the potatoes with the remaining pesto and lightly stir to create a swirl. Serve warm.

Pesto Buttermilk Mashed Potatoes

Gratin Dauphinois

Some of the tastiest things in life are made of a few simple ingredients. Gratin dauphinois is one of those dishes. It consists of just potatoes, cream, cheese, garlic, nutmeg, and butter, with a little salt and fresh cut herbs as garnish. It's not the healthiest dish in the world, but it's well worth the extra calories.

4 tablespoons unsalted butter
2 cloves garlic, finely minced
¾ cup heavy cream
3 Yukon Gold potatoes
¼ cup whole milk

⅛ teaspoon nutmeg, freshly grated
½ teaspoon *fleur de sel*, freshly ground (or regular salt)
¼ teaspoon white peppercorns, freshly ground

3 ounces Gruyère cheese, shredded
1 tablespoon curly parsley, finely chopped

1. **Greasing the dishes:** Preheat oven at 375°F. Grease 6 mini oval gratin dishes with butter, then rub one clove garlic on the bottom and inner sides of the dishes. Pour about 2 teaspoons cream in the bottom of each dish so the potatoes don't burn.

2. **Preparing the potatoes:** Peel and cut the potatoes into ¹⁄₁₆" thick slices with a mandoline. Place them in a large bowl. Cover with ice water, and let sit for 15 minutes. Drain the potatoes and discard the liquid, removing as much excess water as possible. Pat dry using kitchen towels.

3. **Assembly time:** Spread a layer of potatoes in the bottom of each dish, making sure they're tightly and evenly packed. Arrange them by fanning them for a nice presentation. In a bowl, combine the cream, milk, nutmeg, salt, and pepper. In a small pan, melt 2 tablespoons butter and sauté the remaining garlic until lightly golden. Spread the garlic over the first layer of potatoes in each gratin dish. Sprinkle on a thin layer of Gruyère cheese. Divide and pour in half of the cream mixture over the layered potatoes. Add a second layer of the potatoes, then pour the remaining cream on the new layer. Finish with the rest of the Gruyère cheese. Top with bits of the remaining butter. Bake for approximately 50 minutes. Check for tenderness of the potatoes with a knife. Serve immediately.

Truffle Pommes Purée

YIELDS 8 SERVINGS

You can count on one hand the number of ingredients in these very glamorous mashed potatoes. There are potatoes, of course, plus luxurious truffle butter, cream, and salt. These ingredients, especially the truffle butter, really highlight the elegance that is possible even in a simply presented dish.

1½ pounds russet potatoes
1½ teaspoons sea salt
1 cup heavy cream

1 8-ounce package truffle butter, at room temperature

1. **Boiling the potatoes:** Peel the potatoes, cut them into 2" chunks, and place them in a large pot. Fill it with cold water until the potatoes are barely covered. Bring to a boil over high heat, add 1 teaspoon salt, and reduce the heat to medium-high. Cook for 20–25 minutes, until fork-tender. Remove from the pot and drain thoroughly; allow the potatoes to cool a little.

2. **Making the mashed potatoes:** Place the heavy cream in a saucepan. Bring to a near boil over medium heat, and turn off the heat. Once the potatoes are drained and cool enough to handle, return them to their pot over low heat for a few moments to ensure they're completely dried. Turn off the heat. Using a potato ricer, mash the potatoes. Add the truffle butter, stirring vigorously. Add the warm cream until mixture reaches desired consistency.

3. **Assembly time:** The secret to an incredibly smooth purée is to pass it through a coarse-mesh strainer. Take your potato mixture, and press it through the mesh strainer using a silicon spatula. Season with salt to taste. Pepper isn't necessary, as it might overpower the subtle truffle flavor. Serve immediately.

REHEATING MASHED POTATOES
If you reheat mashed potatoes, it's preferable to use a double boiler. If you don't have a double boiler, you can improvise by placing the mashed potatoes in a heatproof bowl over a smaller-sized saucepan filled with simmering water. Add a little kitchen towel underneath the bowl so it won't jiggle and water won't splash into the mashed potatoes. Add up to ¼ cup warm milk to soften and thin the texture, if needed.

Moussaka

YIELDS 10 SERVINGS

Moussaka is a one-dish meal composed of grilled eggplant slices, layers of sliced potatoes, ground spiced lamb, and a creamy béchamel topping. The dish is prepared from Greece through the Balkans and all the way into the Middle East. Variations include a variety of roasted vegetables, and I have also tried one version where the béchamel sauce was replaced with mashed potatoes. Once you're comfortable with the basics of the recipe, have fun and be creative!

3 eggplants
1 tablespoon kosher salt
½ cup olive oil
1 yellow onion, thinly sliced
¼ teaspoon red chili flakes
½ teaspoon ground cinnamon
2 cloves garlic, finely minced
1 pound ground lamb
2 tablespoons tomato paste
1 teaspoon honey

1 tablespoon Worcestershire sauce
½ cup dry white wine
8 tablespoons unsalted butter
2 teaspoons oregano, chopped
¾ cup all-purpose flour
5 cups milk, warmed
¼ cup freshly grated kefalograviera cheese (or pecorino cheese)
½ teaspoon nutmeg, freshly grated
2 teaspoons salt

¾ teaspoon black pepper, freshly cracked
4 white potatoes
3 tomatoes, sliced
¾ cup feta cheese, crumbled
1 tablespoon bread crumbs, freshly ground (for recipe, see Chapter 3, Cheesy Potato Croquettes)
3 tablespoons flat-leaf parsley, chopped

1. **Boiling the potatoes:** Peel the potatoes, cut them into 2" chunks, and place them in a large pot. Fill it with cold water until the potatoes are barely covered. Bring to a boil over high heat, add 1 teaspoon salt, and reduce the heat to medium-high. Cook for 20–25 minutes, until fork-tender. Remove from the pot and drain thoroughly; allow the potatoes to cool a little.

2. **Making the mashed potatoes:** Place the heavy cream over high heat in a saucepan. Bring to a near boil and turn off the heat. Once the potatoes are drained and cool enough to handle, return them to their pot over low heat for a few moments to ensure they're completely dried. Turn off the heat. Using a potato ricer, mash the potatoes. Add the truffle butter, stirring vigorously. Add the warm cream until you reach your desired consistency.

3. **Grilling the eggplants:** Trim the eggplants and slice lengthwise into 5–6 pieces (about ½" thick), depending on the size of the eggplant. Layer a cooling rack on top of a cookie sheet.

Place the eggplant slices on the rack, sprinkle with the kosher salt, and let sit for 20 minutes. Pat dry using a paper towel. Heat a griddle pan over medium heat and brush it with 1 tablespoon olive oil. Drizzle 2 tablespoons oil on the eggplant slices and place them on the griddle. Cook on medium heat until you get grill marks and the eggplant is softened, 3–4 minutes on each side. Remove from the pan and set aside.

4. **Cooking the meat:** Preheat the oven to 350°F. Heat 4 tablespoons oil over medium-high heat in a large, deep pan. Add the onion and cook for 8 minutes, until golden brown. Increase the heat to high heat and add the red chili flakes, cinnamon, and garlic. Cook until fragrant. Add the ground lamb, stirring until the meat changes color. Season with ½ teaspoon salt then add the tomato paste, honey, Worcestershire sauce, and dry white wine. Cover, decrease the heat to medium-low, and cook for 5 minutes. Simmer until a little of the liquid evaporates and the mixture becomes thicker; an additional 5 minutes.

5. **Making the béchamel sauce:** In a saucepan, melt the butter over medium-low heat so it won't burn. Add the oregano. Bring the heat back up to medium-high and add the flour. Stir constantly with a whisk for approximately 3 minutes. The flour should absorb the butter and form a paste. Add the warmed milk in 3 stages, and stir well until fully incorporated. Increase the heat to high while constantly stirring for 5 minutes. Reduce the heat to low, add 2 tablespoons kefalograviera cheese and the nutmeg. Remove from heat. Season with ½ teaspoon salt and ¾ teaspoon pepper. The sauce will become thicker as it cools.

6. **Assembly time:** Brush a 2-quart casserole dish with 1 tablespoon olive oil. Spread a thin layer of the ground lamb into the casserole dish. Cover with half the eggplant slices. Add a layer of sliced potatoes. Cover with fresh tomatoes and the remaining lamb mixture. Sprinkle with crumbled feta cheese. Continue layering the remaining eggplant slices. Cover the dish with the béchamel sauce. Sprinkle with the bread crumbs and the remaining kefalograviera cheese. Place the casserole dish on a baking pan. Bake uncovered for 40–45 minutes. At the end of the cooking time, change the oven setting to broil for 2–3 minutes. Remove from the oven, sprinkle with parsley, and let cool for at least 15 minutes. Serve warm.

Moussaka

Pommes Biarritz

YIELDS 6 SERVINGS

Biarritz is a popular and elegant beach resort for Parisians, less than ninety minutes from the city, in the Basque coast region of France. If you take a trip there, you'll most certainly encounter this potato dish made with cooked ham, bell peppers, and fresh fines *herbes. And if you haven't made the journey yet, you can pretend by cooking this ultra-easy dish.*

3 small bell peppers (1 red, 1 green, 1 yellow), roasted whole, then seeded and diced

7 new potatoes

2¼ teaspoons salt, to taste

¼ cup olive oil, to taste

6 ounces cooked ham, diced

4 tablespoons fresh *fines herbes*, chopped

4 tablespoon unsalted butter, at room temperature

1 cup heavy cream

½ teaspoon nutmeg, freshly grated

½ teaspoon white pepper, freshly ground

1. **Roasting the bell peppers:** Preheat the oven to 450°F. Place the whole peppers on a baking sheet and roast them for 4–6 minutes, until the skins blister and darken, rotating the pan halfway through the roasting process. Watch carefully, so they don't burn. Take them out of the oven, then wrap each pepper in aluminum foil, or seal them in a plastic bag. Let cool for 5–10 minutes, until you can handle them without discomfort. Clean and remove the skin from the peppers with a knife or under running water; the skin will come right off. Seed and dice them.

2. **Preparing the potatoes:** Scrub and peel the potatoes, then place them whole in a large pot. Fill it with cold water until the potatoes are barely covered. Bring to a boil over high heat, add 1 teaspoon salt, and reduce the heat to medium-high. As soon as the water reaches a boil, cook for 25–30 minutes until slightly tender but still firm. Drain the potatoes thoroughly, without rinsing, and let them cool a little.

3. **Assembly time:** In a large saucepan, heat the oil. Add the cooked ham, diced roasted bell peppers, and 2 tablespoons *fines herbes*. Stir well for 2 minutes, then transfer to a plate, leaving as much oil as possible in the pan. Pour out the oil in the saucepan. Add the potatoes over low heat for a minute or two. Coarsely mash them with a potato masher, leaving a few potato chunks for texture. Add the butter and cream until you reach the desired consistency. Add the nutmeg and season with salt and pepper. Return the ham and bell pepper mixture to the saucepan. Mix well. Finish with the remaining *fines herbes*.

Pommes Biarritz

Pommes Mousseline

YIELDS 6 SERVINGS

Pommes mousseline is the airy, light version of mashed potatoes. Whipped cream and eggs ensure that the texture is lump-free and silky. This dish is exceptionally indulgent because of the high ratio of butter and cream to potato, so save this for a special occasion when you don't mind the extra calories!

2½ pounds fingerling potatoes	8 tablespoons unsalted butter, at room temperature	½ teaspoon white pepper, freshly ground
2 teaspoons salt, to taste	½ teaspoon nutmeg, freshly grated	2 egg yolks
2 cups cream, to taste		

1. **Boiling the potatoes:** Scrub the potatoes. Place them whole and unpeeled in a large nonstick pot. Add cold water until the potatoes are barely covered. Bring to a boil over high heat, add 1 teaspoon salt, and reduce the heat to medium-high. As soon as the water boils, cook for 25–30 minutes, until tender. Remove from the pot. Drain the potatoes thoroughly and let them cool a little, but do not rinse.

2. **Making the mashed potatoes:** Warm 1 cup cream for a few minutes in a saucepan over low heat. Meanwhile, mash the potatoes through a potato ricer. For a smooth and silky texture, pass through a large coarse sieve, pushing the potatoes through with a silicone spatula. Add 4 tablespoons butter, nutmeg, the warm cream, and white pepper. Stir vigorously. Return the potatoes to the nonstick pot over very low heat. Add the remaining butter. In a separate bowl, beat the egg yolks. Add 2 tablespoons mashed potatoes to the eggs. Stir until combined. Add 2 more tablespoons mashed potatoes and stir again. A small amount of potatoes is added at a time to prevent the eggs from curdling. Transfer the egg mixture to the pot, stirring constantly. Season with additional nutmeg, salt, and pepper to taste. Turn off the heat.

3. **Assembly time:** Using an electric handheld blender, whip the remaining cream (at a low speed) for approximately 2 minutes, until creamy and frothy. Increase the speed of your mixer and keep beating for another 2–3 minutes until it forms soft peaks. Using a silicone spatula, mix ⅓ of the whipped cream with the mashed potatoes to soften the mixture. Add the rest of the whipped cream and gently fold into the potatoes to get an airy result. Adjust seasoning to taste.

Sweet Mashed Potatoes with Maple Syrup Roasted Bananas

YIELDS 8 SERVINGS

The mild sweetness of this mashed potato dish contrasts well with many savory main courses, especially fish. Maple roasted bananas enhance the sweetness, without being overly sugary. Since sweet potatoes can be a bit watery, this recipe contains one part russet potato to two parts sweet potatoes for a denser texture.

4 pounds sweet potatoes
2 bananas
⅓ cup maple syrup
2 pounds russet potatoes
1¾ teaspoons salt

1½ tablespoons butter
1 cup milk
1 tablespoon flat-leaf parsley leaves, finely chopped
1½ tablespoons Dijon mustard

½ teaspoon white pepper
1 cup heavy cream, warmed 1 minute in the microwave
¾ teaspoon nutmeg, freshly grated

1. **Steaming the sweet potatoes:** Preheat the oven to 350°F. Peel the sweet potatoes and cut them into 1½" pieces. Using a pot with a steamer insert, add cold water until it barely touches the steamer. Place sweet potato pieces in the steamer, bring the water to a boil over high heat, and reduce the heat to medium-high. Steam for approximately 15 minutes, until tender. Once the sweet potatoes are drained thoroughly and cool enough to handle, transfer to a baking pan lined with parchment paper.

2. **Baking the sweet potatoes and bananas:** Using a paring knife, create a 4" long incision in the unpeeled bananas. Drizzle the inside of the bananas with 1 tablespoon maple syrup. Set aside. Drizzle 2 tablespoons maple syrup over the sweet potatoes. Roast the sweet potatoes for 20–25 minutes. Halfway through the baking process, gently toss the sweet potatoes and place the bananas in the middle of them on the pan. Drizzle the remaining maple syrup over the sweet potatoes. Cook for another 20 minutes, until the bananas are tender and juicy and the sweet potatoes are very soft. Keep warm.

3. **Boiling the russet potatoes:** Peel the potato, cut it into 2" chunks, and place them in a large pot. Fill it with cold water until the potatoes are barely covered. Bring to a boil, add 1 teaspoon salt, and reduce the heat to medium-high, so that the potatoes don't fall apart. Cook for 20–25 minutes. The potatoes should be fork-tender. Remove from the pot and drain; allow the potatoes to cool.

4. **Making the mashed potatoes:** In a separate deep saucepan or in the microwave, melt 1 tablespoon butter with the milk over very low heat. Do not boil. The milk should be warm. Once the potatoes are drained and cool enough to handle, return them to their pot for 2–3 minutes over low heat, to ensure they are as dry as possible. Turn off the heat. Using a food mill (or a potato masher), mash the potatoes. Slowly add the warm milk and butter mixture. Stir well, using a wooden spoon. Add the parsley and mustard. Season with ¾ teaspoon salt and ½ teaspoon pepper.

5. **Assembly time:** Scoop and gather the flesh of the bananas into a food mill (or food processor). Add the sweet potatoes, the drippings from the pan, and the warmed heavy cream. Pass them through until smooth. Strain the pulp through a large-mesh sieve, using a silicone scraper to press through as much as possible. Discard the fibrous solids. Combine the sweet potatoes, mashed potatoes, nutmeg, and the remaining butter. Stir to combine. Adjust seasoning, if necessary. Serve warm. Garnish with a sprig of parsley.

Mashed Purple Potatoes
with Herb Goat Cheese

Purple Peruvian fingerling potatoes are used for these mashed potatoes. They're small-sized waxy potatoes, with a skinny, oblong shape. The flesh is dark violet blue surrounded with a white rim. Peruvian fingerlings have a different flavor from regular potatoes, so you'll be surprised how unusual this simple mashed potato dish can seem.

1 pound purple Peruvian fingerling potatoes	¾ cup heavy cream, warmed	½ cup milk, warm, as needed
1 teaspoon salt	½ teaspoon white pepper, freshly ground	2 tablespoons herbed goat cheese, crumbled (optional)
9 tablespoons salted butter, diced and softened to room temperature	2 teaspoons fresh dill, chopped (optional)	

1. **Boiling the potatoes:** Wash the potatoes and place them whole and unpeeled in a large saucepan. Add cold water until the potatoes are barely covered. Bring to a boil over high heat, add 1 teaspoon salt, and reduce the heat to medium-high. As soon as the water reaches a boil, cook for 15–20 minutes, until fork-tender. Remove from the pot. Drain the potatoes thoroughly and let them cool a little, but do not rinse. Once the potatoes are drained thoroughly and cool enough to handle, gently remove the skin using a paring knife.

2. **Assembly time:** Return the potatoes to their saucepan over low heat for a few moments to be sure they're completely dried. Mash the potatoes with a potato ricer. Add the butter, warm cream, white pepper, and 1 teaspoon dill (if using). Stir well. Pass the potato mixture through a coarse-meshed sieve using a silicone scraper. Add 1 tablespoon goat cheese (if using) and warm milk until you reach the desired consistency. Garnish with a small piece of goat cheese and a bit of dill.

Mashed Purple Potatoes
with Herb Goat Cheese

Ajvar Mashed Potatoes

YIELDS 6 SERVINGS

Flavored with a mixture of roasted bell peppers, eggplant, garlic, and red chili pepper, this mashed potato recipe is as colorful as it is flavorful. And it's a great way to work some additional vegetables into your meal.

1 large eggplant	¼ habanero chili, finely chopped	½ cup heavy cream (or milk)
1½ teaspoons salt	4 roasted bell peppers	¼ cup milk, as needed
3 tablespoons olive oil	½ teaspoon black pepper, freshly ground	10 tablespoons unsalted butter
3 cloves garlic, unpeeled	1½ pounds russet potatoes	

1. **Making the eggplant pulp:** Preheat the oven to 450°F. Cut the eggplant in half lengthwise. Sprinkle with salt. Layer a cooling rack on top of a baking sheet, then place the eggplant halves on top, flesh side down, and set the eggplant aside for 30 minutes. Pat dry with a kitchen towel. Place the 2 pieces of eggplant flesh side down on a greased baking sheet. Drizzle with 1 tablespoon olive oil. Bake the eggplant for approximately 20 minutes. The skin should be black and blistered. Flip the eggplant and top it with the cloves of garlic. Drizzle with more olive oil and bake for 10 more minutes. Remove from the oven, then transfer to a large bowl and cover with aluminum foil. Allow to cool for 10 minutes. Gather all the pulp of the eggplant and finely chop into a thick paste. Discard the skin, stem, and seeds.

2. **Roasting the bell peppers:** Preheat the oven to 450°F. Place the whole peppers on a baking sheet and roast them for 4–6 minutes, until the skins blister and darken, rotating the pan halfway through the roasting process. Watch carefully, so they don't burn. Wrap each pepper in aluminum foil. Let cool for 5–10 minutes, until you can handle them without discomfort. Clean and remove the skin from the peppers with a knife or under running water; the skin will come right off. Seed and dice them.

3. **Making the ajvar:** In a food processor, combine the eggplant pulp, habanero chili, roasted bell peppers, and peeled roasted garlic. Pulse until smooth. Season with salt and pepper to taste.

4. **Boiling the potatoes:** Peel the potatoes, cut them into 2" chunks, and place them in a large pot. Fill the pot with cold water until the potatoes are barely covered. Bring to a boil over high heat, add 1 teaspoon salt, and reduce the heat to medium-high. Cook for 20–25 minutes until

fork-tender. Remove from the pot and drain;
allow the potatoes to cool a little.

5. **Making the mashed potatoes:** Combine
the heavy cream and milk, and warm in a saucepan over low heat. Once the potatoes are drained
thoroughly and are cool enough to handle, return
them to the large pot over low heat for a few
moments to be sure they're completely dried.
Turn off the heat. Using a potato ricer, mash
the potatoes. Add the butter, stirring vigorously.
Add the warm cream and milk, until you reach a
slightly thinner consistency.

6. **Assembly time:** Pass the mashed potatoes and
4–6 tablespoons ajvar (depending on how spicy
you like your dish) through a coarse-mesh sieve to
fluff the potatoes and ensure they are completely
smooth. Serve warm.

Chapter 6

spicy

Forget delicately flavored, subtle dishes. These recipes are bold and unforgettable. From Moroccan tagines to Vietnamese curries, potatoes are often paired with fiery chilies and spices to wonderful effect. The potato acts as a canvas upon which the cumin, turmeric, cardamom, chilies, and other exotic spices are "painted."

Indian dishes are famous for their use of spices and I've included some of my favorites. Jeera Aloo (Indian Potato Curry), or cumin potatoes, is perhaps the quintessential example of the Indian culinary approach to potatoes. When paired with poori (Indian flatbread), it makes an outstanding breakfast combination. Chorizo and Morel Mushroom Filled Samosas are another favorite and I've shared a simple and elegant version made with mini wonton wrappers. Any of these dishes can be made either hotter or milder, depending on your tastes as a chef, so don't be afraid to experiment and determine where your heat tolerances lie.

Panipuri

Biting into your first panipuri is an unforgettable experience. A hollow, crisp semolina puff, called puri, *is filled with boiled cubed potatoes, diced tomatoes, garbanzo beans, chopped red onions, plain yogurt, sweet tamarind chutney, and cilantro chutney. At the very last minute, the little cups are filled with tangy mint water.*

1½ pounds white potatoes
1 teaspoon red chili powder, divided
1 teaspoon ground cumin, divided
½ cup garbanzo beans, drained
¼ cup red onion, chopped
2 teaspoons salt, divided

7 ounces packaged tamarind pulp (95% seedless)
1 cup jaggery (or unrefined palm sugar)
1½" piece peeled ginger
⅛ teaspoon red food coloring powder (optional)
1 tablespoon dried mint leaves

50 panipuri (store-bought)
2 large tomatoes, diced
1 cup plain Greek-style yogurt, whisked
½ cup cilantro chutney (see Aloo Bonda recipe, this chapter)
6 cups tangy mint water (see sidebar)

1. **Boiling the potatoes:** Peel the potatoes, cut them into 2" chunks, and place them in a large pot. Fill it with cold water until the potatoes are barely covered. Bring to a boil over high heat, add 1 teaspoon salt, and reduce the heat to medium-high. Cook for 20–25 minutes until fork-tender. Remove from the pot and drain; allow the potatoes to cool a little. Cut them into ¼" cubes.

2. **Preparing the potatoes:** In a mixing bowl, combine the diced potatoes, ½ teaspoon red chili powder, ½ teaspoon ground cumin, and ½ teaspoon salt. Stir well with a fork, lightly mashing the potatoes. Add the garbanzo beans and red onion. Stir well.

3. **Preparing the sweet tamarind chutney:** Place the tamarind pulp and jaggery in a small saucepan. Cover with 2 cups water. Bring to a boil, then reduce the heat to a gentle simmer for 20 minutes. Stir frequently so the tamarind doesn't stick to the bottom of the saucepan. Strain the thickened mixture through a coarse-mesh sieve, discarding any solids and seeds (this mixture can be stored in the refrigerator for a few months). In a blender, combine the tamarind mixture, ginger, ½ teaspoon red chili powder, ½ teaspoon ground cumin, and red food coloring, if using. Pulse until smooth. Top with crushed dry mint leaves, and mix using a spoon. Adjust seasoning with ½ teaspoon salt and jaggery to taste.

 Panipuri
continued

4. **Assembly time:** Using your fingers, create
a little opening in each puri puff. Fill each puff
with the potato mixture and diced tomatoes.
Spoon the plain yogurt into the cavity, cover with
sweet tamarind chutney and the cilantro chutney
(about 2 teaspoons). As soon as you're ready to
eat, fill each puff with the tangy mint water and
eat immediately.

TANGY MINT WATER   In a bowl, combine
6 cups cold water, ¾ teaspoon ground cumin, 2 tablespoons
dried mint, 1 tablespoon *amchur* (dried mango powder), 1
tablespoon freshly grated ginger, ¼ teaspoon red chili powder,
¼ teaspoon black salt. Whisk well and chill in the refrigerator.
It can be stored for up to a week. Black salt, or "kala namak" in
Hindi, is a pungent seasoning found in South Asian cooking. It
consists of regular table salt combined with sodium sulfate and
other minerals that impart both color and aroma.

Kheema Cutlets

YIELDS 12 APPETIZERS

Many cultures have their own latke look-alikes. What sets this Indian version apart is the spicy ground beef, or kheema, *hidden inside. It's spicy, crispy, and creamy all in the same bite. Though not traditional, these richly spiced potato pancakes, called* cutlets *in Hindi, are served with sour cream in addition to tamarind chutney. Kheema cutlets will take you on a journey you won't want to return from!*

12 red-skinned potatoes
1 pound ground beef
1 tablespoon apple cider vinegar
1 teaspoon salt, divided
¼ teaspoon black pepper
½ cup canola oil

3 tablespoons cilantro, chopped
½ green chili pepper, stemmed, seeded, and finely chopped
½ teaspoons red chili powder
¼ teaspoon cumin seeds
¼ teaspoon coriander seeds

Juice of a lemon, freshly squeezed
2 cups sour cream, as garnish
¼ cup red onion, thinly sliced, as garnish
1 cup imli chutney, as garnish (see sidebar)

1. **Boiling the potatoes:** Wash and place the whole, unpeeled potatoes in a small pot. Add cold water until the potatoes are barely covered. Bring to a boil over high heat, add 1 teaspoon salt, and reduce the heat to medium-high. As soon as the water reaches a boil, cook for 10–15 minutes, until tender. Remove from the pot. Drain the potatoes thoroughly and let them cool a little, but do not rinse. Once the potatoes are cool enough to handle and have dried completely, gently remove the skin with a paring knife and grate them using the largest holes of a box food grater. Gather 6 cups grated potatoes

2. **Making the kheema:** Preheat a nonstick pan over high heat, add the ground beef, and cook for 2–3 minutes. Add the vinegar and season

with ½ teaspoon salt and ¼ teaspoon pepper. Cover and let cook over low heat for 10 minutes, stirring occasionally. Add 3 tablespoons oil, fresh cilantro, and green chili. Mix well. Cook for another 2 minutes.

3. **Making the potato mixture:** In a mixing bowl, combine the grated potatoes, ½ teaspoon salt, red chili powder, cumin and coriander. Mix well. Drizzle with lemon juice. Stir until combined.

4. **Shaping the cutlets:** Divide the potato mixture into 12 equal portions. Form a golf ball–sized amount, then flatten it with your hand. Make a small indent in the center of the cutlet for the kheema. Place a heaping tablespoon of kheema in

the indentation and cover the meat with potato around it, creating a ball. Repeat until all the potato mixture is used. Once the potato balls are formed, delicately flatten them and create potato patties. To help prevent the potato mixture from sticking, wet your hands with a little cold water as you work.

5. **Assembly time:** Heat the remaining oil in a cast-iron pan over high heat for about 2 minutes. When the oil is slightly bubbly, arrange 4–5 patties at a time in the pan, making sure not to overcrowd them. Lower the heat to medium-low, and let cook for 1–2 minutes. When you see the edges start to dry, take a small flat spatula and lift around the edges; they should be golden. Flip them over and cook for another 2 minutes. Repeat the same procedure until all the patties are cooked. Serve with sour cream, sliced red onion, and imli chutney on the side.

IMLI CHUTNEY   In a small saucepan, cover 1 cup peeled, ripe tamarind pods with 4 cups water. Bring to a boil and let simmer for 15 minutes until soft. Drain and discard the liquid. Blend the tamarind pulp with 1½ cups water. Pass the pulp through a medium-mesh sieve. Return the tamarind to a blender. Add 1 clove finely minced garlic, 1 chopped green chili pepper, 1 tablespoon chopped cilantro, and ¼ teaspoon salt. Add cold water and pulse until you reach the desired consistency.

Kheema Cutlets

Masala Potato Chips

YIELDS 8 SERVINGS

If you crave spicy Indian food, these oven-fried masala chips are going to become your new obsession. They take no more than 30 minutes in the oven and the masala spices are absolutely intoxicating.

3 russet potatoes, peeled	⅛ teaspoon cumin seeds	⅛ teaspoon cinnamon, freshly grated
1 lemon, freshly squeezed	⅛ teaspoon coriander seeds	¼ teaspoon red chili powder, to taste
¼ cup canola oil	⅛ teaspoon turmeric	¼ teaspoon saffron threads, for color (optional)
1 teaspoon sea salt, to taste	⅛ teaspoon nutmeg, freshly grated	
2 green cardamom pods	⅛ teaspoon citric acid	
1 clove	¼ teaspoon black pepper, freshly cracked	

1. **Preparing the potatoes:** Preheat the oven to 375°F. Place a baking pan (you could use 2 sheets so you can bake more chips at a time) lined with a sheet of parchment paper in the oven while preparing the potatoes. Slice the potatoes into waffle cuts using a mandoline. Place them in a large bowl. Add the lemon juice and cover them with ice water. Let sit for 15 minutes. Drain the potatoes and discard the liquid, removing as much excess water as possible. Pat dry using kitchen towels. Drizzle the potatoes with 2 tablespoons oil. Sprinkle with ½ teaspoon salt. Toss well. Remove the pan from the oven and generously brush the entire surface with 2 tablespoons oil. Return the pan to the oven for another 2–3 minutes.

2. **Making the masala spice mix:** Extract the seeds from the cardamom pods. Use a mortar and pestle to grind the cardamom seeds. In a small pan, over high heat, dry toast and constantly stir the clove, cumin seeds, and coriander seeds for 2 minutes until fragrant. Remove from the stove and add the turmeric, nutmeg, and citric acid. Transfer to the mortar and pestle with the cardamom. Crush into a fine mill. Sift through a fine-mesh strainer. Transfer back to the mortar and pestle. Add ½ teaspoon sea salt, black pepper, cinnamon, red chili powder, and saffron (if using). Grind into a fine powder. Set aside.

3. **Assembly time:** Remove the pan from the oven and, in batches, line the parchment paper with the potato waffle slices. Make sure to space the chips about 1 inch apart so they don't touch

each other. Place the waffle potato chips back in the oven for 15 minutes, rotating the pan halfway through. Lower the temperature to 350°F. Using tongs, flip each potato slice and bake for an additional 5 minutes. Remove from the oven. Transfer the chips onto paper towel-lined baking sheets. Immediately season both sides of the hot chips with masala mix. Toss well. They will harden as they cool down, becoming wavy chips. Repeat the same procedure, brushing the pan with more oil if necessary, until all the potatoes are used. Store the chips in an airtight container until ready to serve.

Cà Ri Khoai Tây

YIELDS 8 SERVINGS

In this Vietnamese version of Indian curry, seasonal vegetables and potatoes are sautéed and cooked in a mild curry sauce made of coconut milk and various spices. It's typically served on a bed of fragrant jasmine rice, with a piece of baguette or rice vermicelli noodles. This dish makes an excellent lunch for any season of the year!

1 orange or white cauliflower

Juice of 1 lemon

1 stick cinnamon

1 teaspoon black peppercorns

1 tablespoon lemon grass purée (see sidebar)

1 small kaffir lime leaf, torn in half (optional)

2 bay leaves, torn in half

2 cloves

2" chunk galangal (or ginger), lightly bruised

4 cloves garlic, coarsely chopped

2 tablespoons water

5 tablespoons canola oil

3 shallots, chopped

¼ teaspoon turmeric

¼ teaspoon cumin

½ teaspoon ground coriander

¾ teaspoon red chili powder, to taste

1 tablespoon grated palm sugar

2 Yukon Gold potatoes, boiled, skinned, and cut into quarters

1 cup vegetable broth

2 5.6-ounce cans unsweetened coconut milk

1 taro root, peeled, quartered, and fried

1 cup fresh green peas

1 tablespoon kosher salt

1 tablespoon green onions, chopped

1. **Boiling the potatoes:** Brush and wash the potatoes. Place them, whole and unpeeled, into a small saucepan, and fill it with cold water until the potatoes are barely covered. Bring to a boil over high heat, add 1 teaspoon salt, reduce the heat to medium-high, and cook for about 8–10 minutes. Test with a fork; the potatoes should be slightly soft. Remove from the pot. Drain the potatoes thoroughly and let them cool a little; don't rinse them. Once the potatoes are cool enough to handle and have dried thoroughly, remove the skin. Cut them into quarters.

2. **Soaking the cauliflower:** Remove the stem and cut the cauliflower into florets. Place the florets in a bowl, cover them with water, and add the juice of half the lemon to prevent them from turning brown. Stir well. Soak for 5 minutes, then drain.

3. **Preparing the curry flavors:** Gather the cinnamon, black peppercorns, lemon grass purée, kaffir lime leaf, bay leaves, and whole cloves in a large tea bag or in a square of cheesecloth, and tie it with some twine.

4. **Making the galangal garlic paste:** Clean the chunk of galangal or ginger and remove any dirt. Peel the galangal root with the edge of a spoon and finely chop it. Place the chopped galangal and 3 cloves of garlic in a blender or a mortar and pestle, adding approximately 2 tablespoons of water for a smooth mixture. Blend at full speed for 1 minute. Set aside.

5. **Caramelizing the shallots:** In a wok, heat the oil over high heat. Add the shallots and cook until slightly golden. Lower the heat to medium-low and continue cooking until soft and tender, about 6 minutes. Transfer the caramelized shallots to a bowl. Set aside.

6. **Assembly time:** In the same wok, add the remaining minced garlic over high heat. Add the turmeric, cumin, ground coriander, and red chili powder. Mix the thick paste for approximately one minute. Add the filled tea bag, caramelized shallots, palm sugar, potatoes, 1 cup vegetable broth, and 1 can coconut milk. Bring to a boil, then decrease the heat to medium-low and stir with a wooden spoon. Cook uncovered for 5 minutes, add the taro, and reduce the liquid by cooking for approximately 8–10 minutes. The liquid should reduce by half. Add the second can of coconut milk, the cauliflower florets, and green peas. Season with salt. Bring to a boil one last time. Simmer uncovered until the cauliflower is softened. Add the green onions and turn off the heat. Adjust seasoning, if necessary. Cover and let sit until you're ready to serve. Remove and discard the tea bag.

PREPARING LEMON GRASS PURÉE   Wash the lemon grass. Remove the white powder from the leaves. Cut the stalk in half. Crush the younger part with the back of a chef's knife and set it aside (you can use it for making broth). Cut the remainder of the stalk into extremely thin slices. In a mortar and pestle, grind the thin slices of lemon grass, then transfer and mix it in a mini food processor. It should turn into a fine moist powder. Gather 1 tablespoon and store the rest in an ice cube tray in the freezer for future use.

Aloo Bonda

Aloo bonda *literally translates to "potato balls" in Hindi. They're also called* aloo pokora. *Regardless of how you refer to them, the spiced grated potato balls are dipped in chickpea flour batter and after a quick turn in the fryer, they're ready to serve. They're typically served as a snack, but they make wonderful appetizers as well.*

---

1 pound Yukon Gold potatoes
1¾ teaspoons salt
¾ teaspoon red chili powder (to taste)
½ tablespoon jalapeño pepper, finely chopped (to taste)
¾ teaspoon ground coriander

¾ teaspoon garam masala
¼ teaspoon turmeric
2 tablespoons cilantro, chopped
Juice of half a lemon
1½ cups chickpea flour, sifted
⅛ teaspoon baking powder

½ teaspoon cumin seeds, toasted and lightly crushed
1 cup cold water
1 quart peanut oil (or regular vegetable oil), for deep frying, as needed

---

1. **Boiling the potatoes:** Scrub and place the whole, unpeeled potatoes in a small pot. Add cold water until the potatoes are barely covered. Bring to a boil over high heat, add 1 teaspoon salt, and reduce the heat to medium-high. As soon as the water reaches a boil, cook for 10–15 minutes, until tender. Remove from the pot. Drain the potatoes thoroughly and let them cool a little, but do not rinse. Once the potatoes are cool enough to handle and have dried completely, gently remove the skin with a paring knife and grate them using the largest holes of a box food grater.

2. **Seasoning the potatoes:** Gather the grated potatoes in a large mixing bowl. Add ½ teaspoon red chili powder, jalapeño pepper, ½ teaspoon salt, ground coriander, ¼ teaspoon garam masala, ⅛ teaspoon turmeric, fresh cilantro, and lemon juice. Mix well and form 22 2" diameter potato balls.

3. **Making the batter:** In another mixing bowl, stir together the chickpea flour, baking powder, ¼ teaspoon red chili powder, ⅛ teaspoon turmeric, cumin seeds, ½ teaspoon garam masala, and ¼ teaspoon salt. Add 1 cup cold water to the dry ingredients and whisk until incorporated. It should have the consistency of pancake batter.

4. **Preparing the oil:** Line a cooling rack with paper towels and stack on top of a baking sheet. Meanwhile, in a large Dutch oven or regular deep fryer, heat the oil for about 2 minutes over high heat. There should be at least 3" of oil in the pot. Wait until the oil is slightly bubbly and a thermometer registers 345°F–360°F. Test the oil by

dropping a teaspoon of the batter into the hot oil. It should float but not swell.

5. **Frying the aloo bonda:** Place the aloo bonda in the batter. Make sure they're well coated with the batter. Lower the heat in the fryer to medium. Using a fork, pick up one aloo bonda and allow the excess batter to drip back into the batter bowl; placing one aloo bonda at a time in the hot oil, cook up to 5 balls per batch, making sure the fritters don't touch each other while frying. Deep-fry for 4–5 minutes, until golden and crunchy, flipping each piece using a spider skimmer. The fritters will start to pop and increase in volume. Delicately lift each fritter, draining as much oil as possible and transfer them to the cooling rack. Repeat the same procedure for the remaining fritters.

6. **Assembly time:** Serve immediately with various chutneys on the side, such as cilantro tamarind chutney (recipe follows).

CILANTRO TAMARIND CHUTNEY   In a blender or in a large mortar and pestle, combine 2 jalapeño peppers, 2 cloves garlic, 2 tablespoons tamarind concentrate, and ½ bunch cilantro. Add ¼ cup water to thin out the chutney, and season with ¾ teaspoon salt.

Aloo Bonda

Aloo Paratha

YIELDS 10 PIECES

Paratha is an Indian layered flatbread that is often stuffed with vegetables or cheese. Though not as well known in the West as naan is, it is one of the most popular breads on the Subcontinent. The preparation for this aloo paratha recipe is fairly easy. The paratha dough consists of grated potatoes, fine milled durum wheat flour, and several spices. Follow these instructions and you'll be enjoying delicious parathas in the comfort of your home!

2 white potatoes
1½ teaspoons salt
½ teaspoon red chili powder
¼ teaspoon turmeric
1 teaspoon ground coriander

½ teaspoon garam masala
¼ cup cilantro, chopped
1 cup durum wheat flour (*atta* flour), plus ½ cup for dusting
¼ cup room-temperature water

2 tablespoons safflower oil (or regular vegetable oil)
½ cup ghee (clarified butter), melted, as needed

1. **Preparing the potatoes:** Scrub and place whole, starchy, unpeeled potatoes in a small pot. Add cold water until the potatoes are barely covered. Bring to a boil over hight heat, add 1 teaspoon salt, and reduce the heat to medium-high. As soon as the water reaches a boil, cook for 10–15 minutes, until tender when pierced with a fork. Remove from the pot. Drain the potatoes thoroughly and let them cool a little, but do not rinse. Once the potatoes are cool enough to handle and have dried completely, gently remove the skin with a paring knife and grate them using the largest holes of a box food grater. Gather the grated potatoes in a large mixing bowl. Add all the spices, fresh cilantro, and salt. Mix well.

2. **Making the paratha dough:** In the same mixing bowl, add the flour and ¼ cup room-temperature water. Mix well until it forms a stiff, dense dough. Add the oil and knead the dough until it's just combined and smooth; it should resemble pizza dough. Roll the dough into a (about 3" long) log, then slice into 10 equal portions. Cover them with a damp towel so they don't dry out. Dust your work space with a little flour. Flatten each piece, creating a 7" diameter round shape that's about ¼ inch thick. Remove any excess flour. Make sure the disks aren't pierced and don't overwork the dough or the bread won't rise. Cover them again with the damp towel.

Aloo Paratha
continued

3. **Assembly time:** Place a flat nonstick griddle pan over high heat. When the pan is hot, place an aloo paratha on the pan, without any oil or ghee. Lower the heat to medium-low. When the edges start to look dry, flip the paratha. Leave it alone for 1 minute. Using the back of a large spoon, spread the paratha with 1 teaspoon ghee in a circular motion. Flip the paratha one more time and spread the other side with an additional 1 teaspoon ghee. Cook for another 2 minutes until lightly golden. Repeat the same procedure until all the parathas are cooked. Serve immediately with the remaining melted ghee on the side.

Jeera Aloo

Jeera aloo is a potato dish made with spicy cumin gravy. Turmeric powder gives the dish its bright yellow color and, along with the heat from the traditional garam masala, makes this dish the ultimate Indian comfort food. Traditionally, jeera aloo is accompanied with deep-fried flatbread rounds called poori. Poori are absolutely divine, but have to be enjoyed immediately after cooking. The combination is often breakfast fare in India, so consider serving it at your next brunch.

5 medium red-skinned potatoes

¾ teaspoon cumin seeds

½ teaspoon mustard seeds

2 tablespoons fresh curry leaves, torn in half

1 serrano chile, stemmed and cut into thirds

¾ teaspoon red chili powder, to taste

¼ teaspoon cumin, freshly ground

¼ teaspoon turmeric

2½ cups water

1¾ teaspoons salt

2 cups fine durum wheat flour, plus more for dusting

1½ cups canola oil, as needed

1 teaspoon paprika (optional)

¼ teaspoon garam masala

⅛ teaspoon mango powder

2 tablespoons lemon juice, freshly squeezed

1. **Preparing the potatoes:** Wash and peel the potatoes. Slice them in half and cut them into 1½" pieces.

2. **Preparing the spices:** In a small pot, heat 1 tablespoon oil over high heat until just shy of the smoking point. Add the cumin seeds and mustard seeds. When the cumin seeds start popping, after 5–10 seconds, add the curry leaves. Add the potatoes, serrano chile, red chili powder, ground cumin, and turmeric. Stir well. Barely cover the potatoes with 2 cups water. Heat to a boil, add 1 teaspoon salt, cover, and reduce the heat to medium-high. Once the water boils, cook for about 10 minutes until the potatoes are slightly tender but still firm. Set aside until you're ready to serve.

3. **Making the poori:** While the potatoes are cooking, prepare the poori. In a mixing bowl, combine the wheat flour, ¼ teaspoon salt, and ½ cup room-temperature water. Mix well until it forms a stiff, dense dough. Add 1 tablespoon oil. Briefly knead the dough until it's just combined and becomes smooth. Cover with a moist, damp towel so it doesn't dry out. Divide the dough into 15 balls. Dust your work space with a little flour. Flatten each piece, creating a 6" diameter

round shape, about ¼" thick. Remove any excess flour. Make sure the disks aren't pierced, and don't overwork the dough or the *poori* won't expand.

4. **Frying the poori breads:** Line a baking sheet with paper towels. Meanwhile, in a deep fryer, heat the remaining oil for 2–3 minutes over high heat. There should be at least 3" of oil in the pot. Wait until the oil is slightly bubbly. Test the oil by dropping a small piece of dough into the hot oil; it should rise to the surface and sizzle. Lower the heat to medium-high. Place 1 disk at a time in the hot oil. In batches, deep-fry, applying very gentle pressure in the center of the bread using a slotted spoon. A small air bubble will appear in the center; flip the bread, apply a little more pressure on the air bubble with the spoon and the bread will inflate. Fry for about 30 more seconds, until puffy and lightly golden. Delicately lift each *poori*, draining as much oil as possible, and transfer them on to the paper towels. Continue with the remaining disks. After 2–3 minutes, the bread will deflate but will still be soft and delicious for several hours.

5. **Assembly time:** Reheat the potatoes; add the paprika (if using) and garam masala. Simmer for another 5 minutes. Once the liquid is thickened, check the doneness of the potatoes; finish with the mango powder and lemon juice. Adjust seasoning with salt, if necessary. Serve warm with the freshly made poori.

Traditional Samosa

YIELDS 18 MINI SAMOSAS

Samosas are popular Indian snacks. These are stuffed with potatoes, peas, onions, and spices. They're served with mint chutney and date tamarind chutney. Samosas are quintessential party food, so if you like to host theme nights, definitely include them in your next Bollywood-inspired fête.

3 Yukon Gold potatoes
1½ teaspoons salt
4 tablespoons jaggery (or regular sugar)
⅓ cup water
8 dates, pitted and chopped
⅓ cup tamarind concentrate
2 tablespoons date syrup (optional)
¾ teaspoon ground cumin

¾ teaspoon red chili powder
2 quarts peanut oil (or regular vegetable oil) for deep-frying, as needed
½ yellow onion, chopped
1 tablespoon cumin seeds
1 teaspoon mustard seeds
½ cup frozen peas
½ jalapeño pepper, finely chopped

Juice of half a lemon
¼ teaspoon turmeric
¾ teaspoon garam masala
1 teaspoon ground coriander
1 package fresh uncooked tortillas, as needed (see sidebar)

1. **Preparing the potatoes:** Scrub the potatoes, and place them whole and unpeeled in a large pot. Fill it with cold water until the potatoes are barely covered. Bring to a boil over high heat, add 1 teaspoon salt, and reduce the heat to medium-high. As soon as the water reaches a boil, cook for 25–30 minutes until slightly tender but still firm. Drain the potatoes thoroughly, without rinsing, and let them cool a little. Once the potatoes are dried and cool enough to handle, remove the skin and coarsely mash them with a potato masher. For texture, it's important to leave a few potato chunks.

2. **Preparing the date tamarind chutney:** In a non-stick saucepan, dissolve 4 tablespoons

jaggery with 2 tablespoons water over high heat. It's important to carefully watch the *jaggery*; as soon as the edges of the saucepan start caramelizing, immediately lower the heat to medium-low. Don't let the jaggery get too dark brown or it will taste burnt. Add 8 chopped dates, ⅓ cup tamarind concentrate, 2 tablespoons date syrup (if using), ¼ teaspoon red chili powder, ¾ teaspoon ground cumin, and salt. In a mini-blender (or a regular blender if you don't have a mini), mix until smooth and thick. Add 3–4 tablespoons water for a smooth flow.

3. **Cooking the onion:** Heat 1 tablespoon peanut oil in a small pan over low heat. Add the chopped onion and sauté for approximately 3 minutes,

stirring frequently to prevent the onion from burning, until it is tender and shiny. Increase the heat to medium-high. Add the cumin seeds and mustard seeds. When the cumin seeds start popping, after 5–10 seconds, turn off the heat.

4. **Seasoning the potatoes:** Place the coarsely mashed potatoes in a large mixing bowl. Add the greens peas, onion, jalapeño, lemon juice, all the spices, and ½ teaspoon salt. Mix well. Divide the potatoes into 9 equal portions.

5. **Forming the samosas:** Cut the tortillas into quarters, forming triangles. Take one triangle of dough and moisten the edges of the base with water using your finger. Fold the base of the triangle (the long side of the triangle) in half and stick one side to the other with water, overlapping the two to create a small conical shape. Gently press to seal the dough. Place 1 portion of potato mixture in the formed pocket. Pinch in the corners and then fold over the open flap, sealing the base to the top with more water to form a pyramid shape. Make a small fold on both extremities and seal shut each corner, so the samosa doesn't burst in the fryer.

6. **Preparing the oil:** Line a cooling rack with paper towels and place on top of a baking sheet. Meanwhile, in a deep fryer, heat the oil for 2 minutes over high heat until a thermometer registers 345°F–360°F, and the oil is slightly bubbly. There should be at least 4" of oil in the pot. Test the oil by dropping a small piece of tortilla into the hot oil. It should float but not swell.

7. **Frying the samosas:** In batches, place the samosas in the oil, being sure not to overcrowd; reduce the heat to medium-low, then deep-fry for 3 minutes until golden, rotating the pieces so all sides are golden. Using a spider skimmer, lift each samosa, draining as much oil as possible, and transfer to the cooling rack. Continue with the remaining samosas. Serve warm with the date tamarind chutney.

Sᴀᴍᴏꜱᴀ Wʀᴀᴘᴘᴇʀꜱ Uncooked tortillas are available, prepackaged, in most grocery stores. You can use frozen eggroll wrappers instead, but I would advise using them double-layered for samosa wrappers.

Lamb Tagine

YIELDS 6 SERVINGS

Tagine is a Berber dish from North Africa. The spices in Berber cooking are very similar to Indian cuisine, but they incorporate additional sweet flavors, usually in the form of dried fruits. Potatoes act as a binding agent in this dish; their floury texture absorbs the beautiful color from the sauce made with saffron, cinnamon, cumin, and ginger. The sweetness of dried plums, dried apricots, and sun-dried tomatoes finishes the dish.

3 pounds Yukon Gold potatoes, peeled and cubed

1 tablespoon salt

2 cups butternut squash, peeled, seeded, and cubed

4 pounds lamb shanks

½ teaspoon red chili powder

6 tablespoons canola oil (or any neutral oil), as needed

2 yellow onions, 1 coarsely chopped and 1 sliced

½ cup fire-roasted diced tomatoes, canned

1 tablespoon baharat spice mix (see sidebar)

½ cup Greek full-fat plain yogurt

1 14-ounce can low-sodium beef broth

2 cloves garlic, crushed and finely minced

4 dried red chiles

1" chunk fresh ginger, peeled and thinly sliced

2 teaspoons lemon zest, finely chopped

1 bay leaf

1 cinnamon stick, broken in half

4 dried plums, quartered

4 dried apricots, halved

4 sun-dried tomatoes, quartered

¼ teaspoon pepper, freshly cracked

¼ cup date syrup (or honey)

¼ cup green olives, pitted

1 14-ounce can artichoke hearts, drained and quartered

½ teaspoon saffron threads, for color

Juice of 1 lemon

3 tablespoons flat-leaf parsley, chopped

2 tablespoons sunflower seeds

1. **Parboiling the potatoes and butternut squash:** Place the potatoes in a stock pot. Fill it with cold water until the potatoes are barely covered. Bring to a boil over high heat, add salt, and reduce the heat to medium-high. Cook for 3–4 minutes. Add the butternut squash and cook for 5 more minutes. Drain and discard the liquid. Set aside.

2. **Preparing the meat:** Rinse the meat and pat dry. Sprinkle with the red chili powder. In a cast-iron pan, heat 2 tablespoons oil until just shy of the smoking point. Place the lamb shanks in the pan, fat side up. Sear the meat for 2 minutes per side until golden. Do not pierce the meat with a fork; use tongs instead so the meat says moist and tender. Transfer the meat to a platter, leaving as much fat as possible in the pan.

3. **Making the baharat sauce:** Preheat the oven to 375°F. In the same cast-iron pan, heat 2 tablespoons oil. Add the chopped onion. Cook until

lightly browned, about 5–7 minutes. Add ¼ cup diced fire-roasted tomatoes and the baharat spice mix. Cook for another 1–2 minutes, then add the yogurt. Transfer the mixture to a blender; blend on low setting until the sauce is smooth but still thick. Add ¼–½ cup beef broth for a smooth flow. Blend again until combined. Wipe out the pan and add more oil. Add the garlic and the dried chilies. Cook for 2 minutes until fragrant. Add the fresh ginger, lemon zest, bay leaf, cinnamon stick, dried fruits, and the sun-dried tomatoes. Stir well and cook for another 2 minutes. Set aside.

4. **Assembly time:** Place the lamb shanks along with the garlic mixture in the cast-iron pan. Season with salt and pepper, to taste; add the baharat mixture, potatoes, squash, date syrup, and the remaining broth. Seal the cast iron pan with aluminum foil and cover with a lid. Bring to a boil for 3–4 minutes. You should see steam escaping from the pan. Transfer to the oven and bake at 375°F for 45 minutes. Uncover, add the sliced onion, ¼ cup tomatoes, olives, and artichoke hearts. Reduce the heat to 350°F and cook for 45 more minutes, uncovered. Add the saffron, drizzle with the lemon juice, and sprinkle with parsley and sunflower seeds. Cover until you're ready to serve. Stir well. Before serving, remove and discard the cinnamon stick and bay leaf.

BAHARAT   *Barahat* literally means "spice" in Arabic. This North African spice mix is similar to garam masala spice mix, but tangier. In a pan, add ½ teaspoon cumin seeds, 1 teaspoon fennel seeds, 1 whole star anise, 4 cloves, 1½ teaspoons coriander seeds, and the seeds from 3 green cardamom pods. Dry roast over high heat for 2 minutes, and stir constantly. Remove the pan from the stove and add ¼ teaspoon freshly grated nutmeg, 1 teaspoon paprika, ½ teaspoon cayenne, 1 teaspoon garlic powder, 1 teaspoon ground ginger, and 1 teaspoon turmeric. Put the spice mix in a grinder and grind the mixture into a fine powder. Sift the powder through a strainer. Store in an airtight container up to 1 month.

Chorizo and Morel Mushroom Filled Samosa

YIELDS 9 SAMOSAS

These samosas are a fusion of cuisines; they're filled with mashed potatoes, morel mushrooms, puréed corn, onion, and spicy chorizo sausage. Dipped in a little crème fraîche to balance the spicy flavors, they make a most satisfying snack.

3 Yukon Gold potatoes
1½ teaspoons salt
½ yellow onion, chopped
2 quarts peanut oil (or regular vegetable oil) for deep frying, as needed
½ cup corn kernels, thawed
Juice of half a lemon

1 tablespoon Tabasco sauce
1 tablespoon cumin seeds
1 teaspoon mustard seeds
1 teaspoon ground coriander
½ teaspoon ground celery seeds
1 teaspoon paprika
4 ounces spicy chorizo sausage

1 clove garlic, finely minced
1 cup fresh morel mushrooms, coarsely chopped
2 tablespoons curly parsley, chopped
18 frozen eggroll wrappers
1 cup crème fraîche

1. **Preparing the potatoes:** Scrub the potatoes, and place them whole and unpeeled in a large pot. Fill it with cold water until the potatoes are barely covered. Bring to a boil over high heat, add 1 teaspoon salt, and reduce the heat to medium-high. As soon as the water reaches a boil, cook for 25–30 minutes until slightly tender but still firm. Drain the potatoes thoroughly, without rinsing, and let them cool a little. Once the potatoes are dried and cool enough to handle, remove the skin and coarsely mash them with a potato masher. For texture, leave a few potato chunks.

2. **Cooking the onion:** Heat 1 tablespoon oil in a nonstick pan over low heat. Add the chopped onion and sauté for 7–8 minutes, stirring

frequently to prevent burning, until the onion is golden. Transfer the onion to a plate, leaving as much oil as possible in the pan.

3. **Puréeing the corn:** Place the corn in a mini food processor and pulse until puréed.

4. **Seasoning the potatoes:** Place the coarsely mashed potatoes in a large mixing bowl. Add the corn, onion, lemon juice, Tabasco sauce, all the spices, and salt. Mix well.

5. **Preparing the chorizo:** Remove the casing from the sausage and crumble the meat. In the same pan that you cooked the onion, add the garlic and cook for about 2 minutes, until fragrant.

Add the chorizo and cook for 2–3 minutes until the sausage has caramelized bits. Add the mushrooms and cook for 2–3 minutes. Add the parsley. Stir and transfer to the potato mixture. Mix until the chorizo is spread evenly (but don't overmix, you want to be able to see pieces of coarsely mashed potatoes and chorizo). Divide the mixture into 9 equal portions.

6. **Forming the samosas:** Cut the eggroll wrappers into triangles and double layer them on top of each other to make the samosa sturdier. Pull one corner along the base of the triangle to the midpoint of the opposite side of the triangle. Hold it in place, and then pull the other corner to the top corner of the triangle, creating a funnel. Make sure that there is no hole at the bottom of your funnel, so the potato filling doesn't leak out. Place about 3 tablespoons of potato mixture in the formed pocket. Fold over the open flap, sealing the base to the top with more water to form a pyramidal shape. Pinch in the corners so the samosa doesn't open in the fryer.

7. **Preparing the oil:** Line a cooling rack with paper towels and place it on top of a baking sheet. Meanwhile, in a deep fryer, heat the oil for about 2 minutes over high heat, until a thermometer registers 345°F–360°F, and the oil is slightly bubbly. There should be at least 4" of oil in the pot. Test the oil by dropping a small piece of wrapper into the hot oil. It should float but not swell.

8. **Assembly time:** In batches, place the samosas one at a time in the oil, being sure not to overcrowd. Reduce the heat and deep-fry for 3 minutes until golden, rotating the pieces so all sides are golden and crispy. Using a spider skimmer, lift each samosa, draining as much oil as possible, and transfer to the cooling rack. Repeat the procedure until all samosas are cooked. Serve warm with crème fraîche on the side.

Aloo Tikki Chaat

YIELDS 8 SERVINGS

Aloo tikki chaat is another popular Indian snack dish. It consists of a bed of thin sev (spiced, crispy lentil noodles) and layers of pan-fried potatoes, covered with plain yogurt, tamarind chutney, cilantro chutney, and a sprinkle of lightly crushed panipuri.

1½ pounds white potatoes

1½ teaspoons salt

1 tablespoon cilantro, chopped

1½ teaspoons red chili powder, to taste

1 teaspoon ground cumin

¾ teaspoon black salt

1 teaspoon paprika

1 teaspoon ground coriander

2 tablespoons canola oil

3 cups mirchi masala thin sev (see sidebar)

2 large tomatoes, diced

1 cup Greek-style yogurt, whisked

1 cup sweet tamarind chutney (see Panipuri recipe, this chapter)

½ cup cilantro chutney (see Aloo Bonda recipe, this chapter)

5 panipuri (store-bought), coarsely crushed

6 cups tangy mint water (see Panipuri recipe, this chapter)

1. **Boiling the potatoes:** Brush and wash the potatoes. Place them, whole and unpeeled, into a small saucepan, and fill it with cold water until the potatoes are barely covered. Bring to a boil over high heat, add 1 teaspoon salt, and reduce the heat to medium-high. As soon as the water reaches a boil, cook for about 8–10 minutes. Test with a fork; the potatoes should be slightly soft. Remove from the pot. Drain the potatoes thoroughly and let them cool a little; don't rinse them. Once the potatoes are cool enough to handle and have dried thoroughly, remove the skin. Cut them into ¼" cubes.

2. **Making the potato mixture:** In a mixing bowl, combine the diced potatoes and cilantro. Add 1 teaspoon red chili powder, ½ teaspoon ground cumin, and ½ teaspoon salt. Stir well with a fork, lightly mashing the potatoes. Wet your hands with water to prevent the potatoes from sticking, and form 24 (approximately 2"-diameter) potato patties. Heat the oil in a nonstick pan over high heat for about 2 minutes. When the oil is hot, arrange 6–7 patties at a time in the pan, depending on how much space you have. Lower the heat to medium-low. Cook for 1–2 minutes per side until lightly golden. Transfer to a cooling rack. Repeat the same procedure until all the patties are cooked.

3. **Making the chaat masala:** In a small bowl, combine the black salt, ½ teaspoon red chili powder, ½ teaspoon cumin, paprika, and coriander. Mix well.

Aloo Tikki Chaat

continued

4. **Assembly time:** Cover a large, flat serving
platter with sev. Top with the diced tomatoes.
Cover with the potato patties and sprinkle with
the chaat masala mix. Spoon the plain yogurt
over; cover with the sweet tamarind chutney and
then spoon on the cilantro chutney. Garnish with
the crushed panipuri.

SEV   The texture of sev noodles resembles potato chips.
You can find these noodles in most Indian specialty markets.

Aloo Tikki Chaat

Chapter 7

sweet

Showing their true versatility, potatoes—particularly sweet potatoes—can be used in desserts as well as for savory dishes. Most people are already familiar with the Southern classic, sweet potato pie, but potatoes can also be used in cakes, custards, and many other unexpected desserts. There's an earthy quality to sweet potatoes that gives an added complexity to any treat. The key is to minimize the fibrous quality of sweet potatoes; proper cooking and straining can solve that.

Like potatoes, sweet potatoes come in many varieties, and I've used several in this chapter. Japanese white sweet potatoes, in particular, are ideal in situations where the flavor of sweet potatoes is desired, but not the color, as in the Japanese White Sweet Potato Tiramisu recipe. In other dishes, such as Lavender Peruvian Purple Potato White Chocolate Torte, the brilliant color may be what makes the dish. In either case, the sweet potato will add a new dimension to even the most familiar of desserts, and will surely have you begging for more!

Lavender Peruvian Purple Potato White Chocolate Torte

YIELDS 6 SERVINGS

Even though Peruvian purple fingerling potatoes are not technically a sweet potato, they work well in this chocolate torte for both their texture, which nicely thickens the luscious dessert, and for their color, which matches the floral flavoring of the dessert: lavender.

2 purple Peruvian fingerling potatoes	10 tablespoons unsalted butter	⅛ teaspoon salt
10 ounces white chocolate	2 egg yolks	1 10" frozen puff pastry (store-bought)
½ cup heavy cream	1 tablespoon granulated sugar	2 whole eggs, separated
2 tablespoons fresh lavender	⅛ teaspoon lavender extract	2 teaspoons powdered sugar, for dusting
¼ cup all-purpose flour	1 teaspoon vanilla extract	

1. **Boiling the potatoes:** Scrub and place the whole, unpeeled potatoes in a small pot. Add cold water until the potatoes are barely covered. Bring to a boil over high heat, then reduce the heat to medium-high. As soon as the water boils, cook for 10–15 minutes until tender. Drain the potatoes thoroughly and let them cool a little, but do not rinse. Once the potatoes are cool enough to handle and have dried completely, gently remove the skin with a paring knife and grate them using the largest holes of a box food grater.

2. **Making the lavender-flavored cream:** Break up the white chocolate bar and finely chop it. In a saucepan, combine the cream and 1 tablespoon lavender over high heat. Bring it to a near boil. Turn off the heat immediately and add the chocolate pieces and 10 tablespoons butter. Using a spatula, keep stirring until the chocolate is fully incorporated and smooth. Strain through a fine mesh and discard all the lavender bits.

3. **Preparing the pie pan:** Preheat the oven to 375°F. With a rolling pin, roll the dough between 2 sheets of parchment paper and place in an 8" deep-dish pie pan lined with one of the parchment paper sheets. Following the curve of the mold, crimp the dough against the edge. Gently press the dough with your fingers so there are no air bubbles. Leave a little excess above the edge, because the dough will settle a bit in the oven. Prick the dough all over with a fork. Chill in the refrigerator for 20–30 minutes.

4. **Preparing the batter:** In a mixing bowl, whisk the 4 egg yolks with sugar until they become pale yellow. Add the lavender extract if using and vanilla extract. Stir well. Combine the

potatoes with the egg mixture. Mix until combined, then slowly add a ladle of the lavender-flavored cream at a time to prevent the yolks from curdling. In another bowl, add ⅛ teaspoon salt to the egg whites. Beat them for 2 minutes at medium speed. Increase to the maximum speed and keep beating for another 2–3 minutes until the whites are frothy. Pour ⅓ of the egg white mixture into the potato mixture and gently stir everything to soften the batter. Pour in the remaining egg whites and, using a spatula, gently fold the egg whites into the potatoes to get an airy batter. Fill the tart pan with the cake batter and bake for 20–25 minutes until the torte puffs slightly. Check for doneness. A skewer or a toothpick inserted into the center of the torte should come out clean.

5. **Making the lavender sugar:** Using a mortar and pestle, grind 1 teaspoon lavender with the powdered sugar.

6. **Assembly time:** Dust the torte with the lavender sugar. Serve the warm torte with a dollop of sweetened whipped cream or a scoop of vanilla ice cream.

LAVENDER   If you don't have fresh lavender, you can substitute 1 tablespoon dried lavender or 1 tablespoon lavender extract. The lavender reinforces the color of the potatoes and adds a pleasant fragrance to the white chocolate torte.

Lavender Peruvian Purple Potato
and White Chocolate Torte

Yam and Semolina Flan with Pistachio Spun Sugar

YIELDS 6 SERVINGS

Semolina flan is a French dessert packed with Oriental spices. Mashed and strained sweet potatoes provide color and a complement to the earthy flavors already present. The creamy dessert itself, though nicely complex, isn't very sweet. The richness of the caramel sauce and the pistachio candied spun sugar garnish are a welcome contrast.

3 cardamom pods	1¼ cups semolina flour	1 yam
2 cups granulated sugar	3 whole eggs, at room temperature	⅛ teaspoon salt
5 tablespoons water	½ teaspoon freshly ground cinnamon	1 tablespoon light corn syrup
4¼ cups whole milk	1½ tablespoons unsalted butter, at room temperature	1½ tablespoons unsalted roasted pistachio kernels, finely crushed
1 vanilla bean		

1. **Extracting the cardamom seeds:** Using a mortar and pestle, pound the pods several times until they open. Keeping the seeds, pick out the pod shells and discard them. Grind the seeds into a fine powder.

2. **Forming the caramel bottom:** Line up 6 ramekins. In a small saucepan, gently dissolve 1 cup sugar with 3 tablespoons water over high heat. Make sure all the sugar is dissolved and that there is none on the side of the saucepan. Bring to a full boil over high heat, then lower to medium-low until the caramel becomes golden brown, about 5–6 minutes. Immediately pour a layer of caramel into each ramekin.

3. **Steaming the yam:** Peel the yam and cut it into 1½" pieces. Fill a pot with cold water. Add a steamer insert (remove the excess water, if necessary until it barely touches the steamer level), and place yam pieces in the steamer. Bring the water to a boil over high heat, and reduce the heat to medium-high. Steam for approximately 15 minutes, until tender. Once the sweet potatoes are cool enough to handle and have dried with no excess water, transfer to the bowl of your food processor. Pulse until smooth. Strain the pulp through a large-mesh sieve, using a silicone spatula to press through as much as possible. Discard the fibrous solids.

4. **Preparing the vanilla:** Using a paring knife, scrape and gather all the grains of the vanilla bean. Set aside.

5. **Making the flan batter:** In a saucepan, heat the milk. Add the vanilla bean and its grains. Bring to a near boil over high heat. Lower the heat immediately and add the semolina flour. Watch the milk carefully when it comes close to a boil, as it heats quickly and can easily boil over. Using a whisk, stir continuously for 5–8 minutes until the mixture thickens. Pick out and discard the vanilla bean. In a mixing bowl, whisk the eggs with ½ cup sugar until it becomes pale yellow. Add the cardamom and cinnamon. Add the egg mixture to the milk a little at a time to prevent the yolks from curdling. Finish with the yam pulp and butter. Mix well.

6. **Baking the ramekins:** Preheat the oven to 425°F. Fill the 6 ramekins with the mixture. Place them in a warm water bath in a deep baking pan. The water should go halfway up the side of the ramekins. Bake for 30 minutes, until the top is golden. If you plan on serving them warm, hold them for a few minutes in an oven at the lowest setting. If you plan on chilling them, place them in the refrigerator.

7. **Assembly time:** In a small saucepan, combine the remaining ½ cup sugar, corn syrup, and 2 tablespoons water. Stir, using wooden chopsticks or a spoon, and cook over medium-low heat. It will take some time (about 5 minutes) until it becomes a syrupy caramel. Allow to cool for 2–3 minutes. Using the chopsticks, dip and vigorously swirl thin lines of the hot caramel sugar over a sheet of parchment paper or a silicone mat. Immediately sprinkle with some ground pistachios. Let the decoration set, then carefully lift and detach the pretty piece to decorate the flan. Repeat the same procedure for the rest of the ramekins.

Candied Yam Dessert Cup with Chocolate Ginger Mousse, Gingersnap, and Marshmallow Brûlée

This is a truly unique dessert—think candied yams meet s'mores. It's an upscale interpretation in parfait cups with layers of ginger chocolate mousse, gingersnap cookies, and a brûléed marshmallow top. Your guests will think they're eating at a 5-star restaurant!

2 yams	3 tablespoons ginger, freshly grated	12 gingersnap cookies, crushed, reserving 8 for garnish
6 tablespoons butter	6 tablespoons whole milk	1 7-ounce jar marshmallow cream, as needed
5 tablespoons granulated sugar	1 cup semisweet chocolate chips	
2 teaspoons light corn syrup	⅓ cup heavy whipping cream, cold	

1. **Candying the yams:** Preheat the oven to 350°F. Melt 2 tablespoons butter. Peel the yams and cut them into 1½" pieces. Using a pot with a steamer insert, add cold water until it barely touches the steamer. Place yam pieces in the steamer and bring the water to a boil over high heat, and reduce the heat to medium-high. Steam for 10 minutes, until tender. Allow to rest for a few minutes so there is no excess water. Drizzle with 2 tablespoons butter, 2 teaspoons granulated sugar, and the corn syrup. Toss well, transfer to a 1½-quart greased casserole dish. Bake for 20 minutes, then transfer to the bowl of a food processor. Add 1 tablespoon grated ginger and pulse until smooth. Pass the pulp through a large-mesh sieve, using a silicone scraper to press through as much as possible. Discard the fibrous solids.

2. **Making the ginger chocolate mousse:** Place the remaining grated ginger in a piece of fine cheesecloth. Squeeze as much juice as possible into a small bowl (approximately 1 tablespoon), and discard the solids. On the stove, place the milk and remaining sugar in a saucepan. Bring to a near boil over high heat. Turn off the heat and immediately add the chocolate chips and ginger juice. Stir well. Add the remaining butter. Using a spatula, keep stirring until the morsels are melted. Let the mixture cool completely on the stove, stirring the mixture every 15 minutes to keep it from forming a skin. Once cooled, use an immersion handheld mixer to whip the cream at a low speed for approximately 2 minutes, until creamy and smooth. Increase the speed of your mixer and keep beating for another 2–3 minutes until the

Candied Yam Dessert Cup with Chocolate Ginger Mousse, Gingersnap, and Marshmallow Brûlée
continued

cream forms soft peaks. Using a silicone spatula, mix ⅓ of the whipped cream with the chocolate mixture to soften it. Add the rest of the whipped cream and gently fold it into the mousse to get an airy batter.

3. **Filling the cups:** Reserve 8 gingersnap cookies for the final step and crush the rest. Line up small clear cups or glasses. Transfer the mousse to a pastry bag and pipe, or spoon a thin layer of the ginger chocolate mousse into the dessert cups. Add a layer of candied yams. Top with the crushed gingersnap cookies. Leave a little room for the crushed gingersnap cookies and the marshmallow cream. Cover with plastic wrap and place the cups in the refrigerator for at least 2–3 hours so the chocolate can set.

4. **Assembly time:** When serving, unwrap the desserts and fill the top with marshmallow cream. Use a spreader to remove the excess cream. Brûlée the top with a culinary torch until the marshmallow forms a golden brown crust and starts to bubble. The marshmallow will caramelize and can burn fast, so watch it carefully as it changes color until the crust is formed. Garnish with a gingersnap cookie.

Candied Yam Dessert Cup with
Chocolate Ginger Mousse, Gingersnap,
and Marshmallow Brûlée

Japanese White Sweet Potato Tiramisu

The custard in this tiramisu is subtly flavored with mashed Japanese white sweet potatoes and vanilla beans. Separated by coffee-soaked ladyfingers, this parfait tastes as incredible as it looks.

1 Japanese white sweet potato
1 vanilla bean
3 egg yolks, at room temperature
6 tablespoons superfine sugar
⅛ teaspoon salt

10 ounces mascarpone cheese, softened to room temperature
6 tablespoons powdered sugar
2½ cups heavy whipping cream, cold
2 cups granulated sugar
2 cups water

½ cup Kahlúa (or any coffee liqueur), optional
12 ladyfinger cookies
1 cup espresso coffee
1 tablespoon unsweetened cocoa powder

1. **Steaming the sweet potato:** Peel the sweet potato and cut it into 1½" pieces. Using a pot with a steamer insert, add cold water until it barely touches the steamer. Place the sweet potato in the steamer, bring the water to a boil over high heat, and reduce the heat to medium-high. Steam for 15 minutes, until tender. Once the sweet potato is dried and cool enough to handle, transfer to the bowl of your food processor. Pulse until smooth. Strain the pulp through a large-mesh sieve, using a silicone spatula to press through as much as possible. Discard the fibrous solids.

2. **Preparing the vanilla:** Using a paring knife, scrape and gather all the grains of the vanilla bean. Discard the pod and set aside the grains.

3. **Making the mascarpone filling:** In a stainless-steel mixing bowl, using an electric handheld mixer, at full speed whisk the egg yolks with the superfine sugar until the mixture thickens. Fill a small saucepan with water, cover it with a piece of cloth, and place a heatproof bowl filled with the whisked eggs on top. The bowl should be large enough that it sits on top of the pan and can't fall in. Beat the eggs at full speed for 4–5 minutes. Check the temperature of the eggs; they should feel warm to the touch, and the mixture should fall like a ribbon of sauce when you lift the whisk. Remove from the double boiler; add the vanilla grains and salt. Stir in. Let cool to room temperature, cover with plastic wrap, and refrigerate for at least 30 minutes. In another mixing bowl, whisk the mascarpone cheese with 2 tablespoons powdered sugar to soften it. Slowly add the egg mixture to the mascarpone. Mix well. Add the sweet potato and stir until the mixture is thick but uniform. Clean your handheld mixer in

hot soapy water and finish with cold water so the blades are cold. (Always be sure that beater blades are completely clean prior to whipping cream for optimum results.) Whip the cold cream at low speed for 2–3 minutes until creamy and smooth. Add the rest of the powdered sugar. Increase to maximum speed and keep beating for another 2–3 minutes, until it forms soft peaks. Pour ⅓ of the whipped cream into the mascarpone cream. Mix well with a silicone spatula. Pour in the rest of the whipped cream; gently fold in the whipped cream to get an airy mousse.

4. **Preparing the coffee syrup and the ladyfingers:** Make a syrup by combining the granulated sugar and 2 cups water in a large saucepan. Stir well. Bring to a boil and add the espresso coffee to the syrup. Finish with the Kahlúa liqueur (if using). Stir well again and then let the syrup cool down for at least 15 minutes. Soak the ladyfinger cookies in the syrup for a maximum of 2½ minutes. The cookies should absorb the coffee syrup but should not be soggy. Using forks, transfer the cookies directly onto the bottom of a 9" square springform pan lined with parchment paper.

5. **Assembly time:** Cover the soaked ladyfingers with the mascarpone cream. Repeat with another layer of ladyfingers and mascarpone cream. Level the filling with a spatula. Carefully plastic-wrap and place in the refrigerator for at least 6 hours. When you're ready to serve, unwrap the pan, unmold the dessert, and sprinkle with cocoa powder.

Sweet Potato and Matcha Green Tea Crème Brûlée

YIELDS 8 SERVINGS

The natural jade color of matcha green tea powder, along with its distinctive flavor, makes this crème brûlée a truly gourmet dessert. There's something special about the flavor of green tea that cuts the decadence of the dessert, while enhancing its elegance.

1 Japanese white sweet potato	1⅔ cups white chocolate chips	⅛ teaspoon salt
2¼ cups heavy cream	4 egg yolks	3 tablespoons matcha green tea powder
¼ cup whole milk	1 teaspoon pure vanilla extract	¼ cup sugar, as needed

1. **Steaming the sweet potato:** Peel the sweet potato and cut it into 1" slices. Using a pot with a steamer insert, add cold water until it barely touches the steamer. Place the sweet potato in the steamer, bring the water to a boil over high heat, and reduce the heat to medium-high. Steam for 15 minutes, until tender.

2. **Making the sweet potato pulp:** Once the sweet potato is dried and cool enough to handle, transfer to the bowl of a food processor. Pulse until smooth. Strain the pulp through a large-mesh sieve, using a silicone spatula to press through as much as possible. Discard the fibrous solids.

3. **Melting the chocolate:** Preheat the oven to 325°F. In a saucepan, combine the cream and milk over high heat. Bring it to a near boil. Watch carefully so that the milk doesn't boil, as the liquid heats very quickly. Turn off the heat; immediately add the white chocolate chips. Using a spatula, keep stirring until the morsels are fully incorporated and melted. Strain the warm liquid through a fine-mesh sieve. Set aside.

4. **Making crème brûlée:** In a mixing bowl, whisk the egg yolks with 6 tablespoons sugar until the mixture becomes pale yellow. Add the vanilla extract, salt, and matcha green tea powder. Add the egg mixture to the chocolate mixture a little at a time to prevent the yolks from curdling. Stir until just combined. Strain through a medium-mesh sieve to eliminate any chunks of chocolate, milk skin, or fibrous parts of the sweet potato.

5. **Arranging the custards:** Fill 8 heat-proof Japanese tea cups with the custard. Place them in a warm water bath in a deep baking pan. The

water should go halfway up the side of the cups, at least 1½" high. Loosely cover the pan with a sheet of aluminum foil and place in the oven for 30–35 minutes. Open the oven and remove the aluminum foil; continue cooking for another 5 minutes. The texture should be a little jiggly but not liquid, the custard will get firmer and creamier as it chills in the refrigerator.

6. **Assembly time:** Allow the *crème brûlée* to cool completely, then plastic-wrap the individual cups and chill in the refrigerator for at least 3 hours. When ready to serve, unwrap the tea cups and sprinkle about 1½ teaspoons sugar in each cup. Caramelize with a culinary torch.

Tarte Amandine aux Patates Douces

This French apple dessert is not your average tart. The almond buttercream is flavored with sweet potatoes, which gives a luscious taste and a warm color to the tart filling. To make the dessert look extra fancy without being too complicated, apple slices are arranged in the shape of a flower.

1 medium-size sweet potato	2 tablespoons maple syrup	1 tablespoon raw sugar
8 5"×5" squares frozen puff pastry dough (store-bought)	1 egg, at room temperature	4 Golden Delicious apples
5 tablespoons unsalted butter	¼ cup granulated sugar, to taste	Juice of 1 lemon
¼ teaspoon cinnamon, freshly ground	1 teaspoon pure vanilla extract	¼ cup apricot preserves, as needed
	10 ounces almond flour	⅛ teaspoon salt

1. **Steaming the sweet potato:** Peel the sweet potato and cut it into 1½" pieces. Using a pot with a steamer insert, add cold water until it barely touches the steamer. Place sweet potato pieces in the steamer, bring the water to a boil over high heat, and reduce the heat to medium-high. Steam for approximately 15 minutes, until tender.

2. **Making the sweet potato pulp:** Once the sweet potato is dried and cool enough to handle, transfer to the bowl of your food processor. Pulse until smooth. Strain the pulp through a large-mesh sieve, using a silicone spatula to press through as much as possible. Discard the fibrous solids.

3. **Forming the tart shells:** Preheat the oven to 375°F. Make sure the puff pastry dough is thawed but still cold so it's easy to place in the molds. Place the dough in 8 individual 4" diameter mini pie shells lined with parchment paper. Follow the curve of the molds and crimp the dough against the edges. Gently press the dough with your fingers so there are no air bubbles. Leave a little excess above the edges to allow the dough to settle a bit in the oven. Prick the dough with a fork 3–4 times to let some of the steam escape as it bakes and set aside.

4. **Making the almond buttercream filling:** In a nonstick pan, melt 1 tablespoon butter over medium heat. Add the sweet potato pulp and ground cinnamon. Cook for 4 minutes, until the mixture thickens. Drizzle with 2 tablespoons maple syrup. Stir well. Once the syrup is well combined, turn off the heat and set aside. Using an electric handheld mixer at full speed, whisk

the egg with the sugar until it becomes a pale yellow foam. The consistency should be very airy. It will take 5–6 minutes. Add the vanilla extract, salt, and the sweet potato mixture. Mix well. In a separate bowl, cream 4 tablespoons softened butter. Pour in the egg mixture. Mix well. Add the almond flour and mix until the batter is smooth.

5. **Preparing the apples:** Peel, core, and cut the apples in half. Slice the halves into 4 small wedges. Coat them with lemon juice to prevent them from browning.

6. **Baking the tarts:** Fill the unbaked tart shells with the sweet potato almond buttercream. Smooth the almond cream with a flat spatula. Sprinkle the cream with raw sugar. Top the tarts with the apples, forming a pretty flower shape. Place the apple tartlets on a baking sheet and bake for 10 minutes at 375°F, then lower the temperature to 350°F and bake for another 25–30 minutes. The shell should be flaky.

7. **Assembly time:** At the end of the cooking time, change the oven setting and broil for about 2 minutes. Once the apples are nicely browned, remove them immediately from the oven and brush each tartlet with a thin layer of warm apricot preserves for a nice glossy look. Let the tartlets cool for a few minutes. Remove the shells from the molds. Serve warm with a scoop of vanilla ice cream or a dollop of sweetened whipped cream.

Tarte Amandine aux Patates Douces

Sweet Potato Brioche

YIELDS 12 SERVINGS

Brioche is a mildly sweet French bread made of eggs and butter. This one is flavored with sweet potatoes, which also tint the bread a pretty color. It's a perfect breakfast bread, and it is often used in France to make pain perdu, *or French toast.*

---

1 sweet potato
¼–½ cup reserved sweet potato water, lukewarm
1 cup warmed milk, plus 1 tablespoon (for the egg wash)
1½ packages instant dry active yeast

½ cup granulated sugar
6 cups all-purpose flour
¼ cup dry milk
1½ teaspoons salt
2 whole eggs, 1 whole and 1 separated
1 egg yolk

½ teaspoon vanilla extract
1 tablespoon oil
6 tablespoons unsalted butter, at room temperature, plus extra for the molds
3 tablespoons Belgian pearl sugar (optional)

---

1. **Steaming the sweet potato:** Peel the sweet potato and cut it into 1½" pieces. Using a pot with a steamer insert, add cold water until it barely touches the steamer. Place sweet potato pieces in the steamer, bring the water to a boil over high heat, and reduce the heat to medium-high. Steam for approximately 15 minutes, until tender.

2. **Making the sweet potato pulp:** Once the sweet potato is dried and cool enough to handle, transfer to the bowl of your food processor. Pulse until smooth. Strain the pulp through a large-mesh sieve, using a silicone spatula to press through as much as possible. Discard the fibrous solids. Gather 1 cup of sweet potato pulp.

3. **Dissolving the yeast:** Preheat the oven to 375°F. Warm the milk. The temperature should register between 105°F and 120°F for both the milk and the potato water. In a small bowl, combine the yeast, the warm milk, and 1 teaspoon granulated sugar. Stir a little so the yeast dissolves and let it rest for 10–20 minutes.

4. **Forming the brioche dough:** In a large bowl, sift together 4 cups flour, the dry milk, and the salt. In a separate bowl, using a handheld mixer, whisk 1 whole egg and 2 egg yolks with the remaining granulated sugar until thickened. Add the vanilla extract. Mix well. Lightly oil the bowl of a stand mixer. Place the sifted dry ingredients in the bowl. Form a well. Using the mixer's dough hook, mix the dry mix with half the egg mixture. Add the leavened yeast and milk mixture. Add the sweet potato pulp, the remaining egg mixture and the softened butter. Add 2 tablespoons sweet potato water, up to ½ cup total; the dough should

be soft and a bit sticky. Add 1 tablespoon pearl sugar. Knead the dough until the butter is just fully incorporated.

5. **Resting the dough:** Transfer the dough to a marble pastry board or any clean surface. Knead the dough for about 3 minutes, until it becomes smooth. Don't overwork the dough. Place in a lightly oiled bowl. Drizzle the top with a little oil (approximately 2 teaspoons) to prevent the dough from drying. Cover with a towel and place the bowl in a warm area until doubled in volume, approximately 1½ hours. Do not extend the leavening time more than 2 hours.

6. **Forming brioches à tête:** Lightly grease 12 fluted 3½" individual nonstick brioche molds with a thin layer of butter. Dust your work space and hands with a generous amount of flour and divide the dough into 4-ounce balls. With the side of your hand, make an indentation around the top of each dough ball, creating a little dough ball, about ⅓ the size of the base, which will become the "head" of the brioche à tête. It should resemble a squat bowling pin. Lift it by the "head" and place in the mold. Dust your fingers with more flour. Grab the head and sink it all the way to the bottom of the mold, so it's properly set. Cover

with a towel and place the brioches in a warm area to rest for about ½ hour prior to baking.

7. **Making the egg wash:** Using a fork, beat the remaining egg white with 1 tablespoon milk. Lightly brush the egg wash over the brioches. Make sure to coat the entire outer surface. Sprinkle with pearl sugar.

8. **Assembly time:** Bake for 5 minutes at 375°F, then lower the temperature to 350°F and bake for another 25 minutes until golden. Remove the brioches from the oven. The key to success is to measure the internal temperature to guarantee proper doneness—it should register 205°F. Let them cool for about 5 minutes. Unmold the brioches on a cooling rack. Serve immediately or store in an airtight container up to 2 days.

Potato Beignets with Chestnut Purée Filling

YIELDS 6 SERVINGS

*Beignets are a popular after-school snack in France (*le goûter de quatre heures*). In English, this translates to "the 4 o'clock snack." This version of the moist, soft doughnut is filled with sweet chestnut purée, another popular ingredient among French children.*

---

3 white potatoes

1 whole egg

3 tablespoons granulated sugar

¾ cup all-purpose flour, plus extra for dusting

⅛ teaspoon anise extract (optional)

¼ cup fromage blanc

¾ teaspoon baking powder

2 tablespoons melted butter

⅛ teaspoon salt

½ teaspoon pure vanilla extract

1 quart peanut oil (or regular vegetable oil), for deep frying, as needed

10 ounces chestnut purée (3 100-gram tins), as needed

½ cup powdered sugar, for dusting

---

1. **Boiling the potatoes:** Peel the potatoes and cut them into 2" pieces. Place in a large nonstick pot. Add cold water until the potatoes are barely covered. Bring to a boil over high heat. As soon as the water boils, reduce the heat to medium-high and cook for 25–30 minutes, until tender. Remove from the pot. Drain the potatoes thoroughly and let them cool a little, but do not rinse.

2. **Making the mashed potatoes:** Mash the potatoes through a potato ricer. For a smooth and silky texture, pass through a large coarse sieve, using a silicone scraper to push them through. Gather 1½ cups potatoes.

3. **Making the beignet dough:** In a stainless-steel mixing bowl, using an electric handheld mixer, whisk the egg with the sugar. When the mixture thickens, add 1½ cups potatoes,

all-purpose flour, anise extract (if using), fromage blanc, baking powder, melted butter, salt, and vanilla extract. Mix until just combined. The dough should be smooth and a bit sticky. Do not hesitate to add a bit of milk if it's too dry or more flour if it's too sticky.

4. **Preparing the oil:** Place a cooling rack lined with paper towels on top of a baking sheet. Meanwhile, in a large Dutch oven or regular deep fryer, heat the oil for about 2 minutes over high heat, until a thermometer registers 345°F–360°F. There should be at least 3" of oil in the pot. Test the oil by dropping a teaspoon of the batter into the hot oil. It should float but not swell.

5. **Deep-frying the beignets:** Dust your fingers with a generous amount of flour. Form golf ball–sized amounts of the dough, then flatten

Chapter 7 sweet   183

them between your hands. Even out the size of the beignets using a 1½" scalloped circle cutter. In batches, place the beignets in the hot oil, being sure not to crowd them. The beignets will start to pop and increase in volume. Lower the heat to medium. Deep-fry for 3–4 minutes until both sides are golden brown. Using a spider skimmer, remove the beignets and place them on the cooling rack. Continue until all the beignets are cooked.

6. **Assembly time:** When the beignets are cool enough to handle, fill a piping bag with the chestnut purée and use a very small, narrow attachment tip. Insert the tip into the center of each beignet and fill with 1–1½ teaspoons chestnut purée. Dust them with powdered sugar using a fine-mesh strainer. Serve immediately.

Potato Beignets with Chestnut Purée Filling

Prince William's Cake

YIELDS 8 SERVINGS

This dessert closes our tour around gourmet potato dishes. What better way to conclude it than with a royal dessert? This was inspired by Prince William's groom's cake, which happens to be his favorite: chocolate biscuit cake. Potato biscuits are torn and mixed in a chocolate candy bar–like mixture, topped with sweet potato mousse and chocolate-glazed potato biscuits. Get ready for the most decadent dessert you've ever had!

2 medium or 3 small white potatoes
2 cups all-purpose flour
¾ teaspoon salt
1 cup granulated sugar
1½ teaspoons baking powder
1 teaspoon baking soda
7 tablespoons cold unsalted butter, diced

4 tablespoons vegetable shortening
½ cup milk, plus 3 tablespoons
2 tablespoons buttermilk
1 whole egg
10 ounces semisweet chocolate chips
5 tablespoons orange blossom honey
1½ teaspoons pure vanilla extract

1 purple yam
2 egg yolks, at room temperature
10 ounces mascarpone cheese, softened to room temperature
2¾ cups heavy whipping cream, cold
1 tablespoon powdered sugar, for dusting cake

1. **Boiling the potatoes:** Peel the potatoes and place them whole in a large nonstick pot. Add cold water until the potatoes are barely covered. Bring to a boil over high heat. As soon as the water boils, reduce the heat to medium-high and cook for 30 minutes, until fork tender. Remove from the pot. Drain the potatoes thoroughly and let them cool a little, but do not rinse.

2. **Making the mashed potatoes:** Grate them using the largest holes of a box food grater. For a smooth and silky texture, pass through a large coarse sieve, using a silicone scraper to push them through. Gather 1 cup potatoes.

3. **Forming the biscuit dough:** Preheat the oven to 400°F. Reserve 1 tablespoon flour for rolling the dough on the pastry board. In a bowl, sift together the flour, ½ teaspoon salt, 2 tablespoons sugar, baking powder, and baking soda. In a separate mixing bowl, combine the sifted dry ingredients and the grated potatoes. Grate 2 tablespoons butter over the bowl using a box grater. Add two tablespoons diced shortening. Mix the ingredients with a pastry blender. Once all the butter pieces are coated with flour, add ½ cup milk. Mix until coarsely blended and still crumbly. Incorporate 2 tablespoons buttermilk and the remaining 2 tablespoons shortening to the biscuit mixture. Do not overmix; otherwise the biscuits will have a dense texture. Sprinkle the reserved flour over a pastry

board and transfer the biscuit dough. Using a rolling pin, even out the dough to approximately 1" thickness. Create 28 mini disks using a 1" diameter biscuit cutter, and form the last 2 disks with the remnants of dough, remembering to knead the dough as little as possible.

4. **Making the egg wash:** In a small bowl, beat the egg with 1 tablespoon milk, using a fork. Lightly brush the egg wash over the biscuits. Make sure to coat the entire outer surface.

5. **Baking the biscuits:** Place the biscuits on a baking sheet, lined with a silicone mat. Bake for 20 minutes. Let cool completely. Reserve 6 for garnish, coarsely crumble 8 with your fingers, and save the rest for a different dish.

6. **Making the chocolate ganache:** Make a "double boiler" (a slightly smaller saucepan filled with hot water, covered with a piece of cloth) and place a heatproof bowl containing 6 ounces chocolate chips atop the cloth. Melt 8 ounces chocolate. Add 4 tablespoons butter, 2 tablespoons milk, and 4 tablespoons honey. Remove from the double boiler; add ½ teaspoon vanilla extract. Mix well. Allow to cool for 15 minutes. Gently fold in the crumbled potato biscuits. Transfer to a 9" square

springform pan lined with plastic wrap. Level the filling with a spatula. Carefully cover with plastic wrap and place in the refrigerator for at least 3 hours.

7. **Steaming the yam:** Peel the yam and cut into 1½" pieces. Using a pot with a steamer insert, add cold water until it barely touches the steamer. Place the yam in the steamer basket, bring the water to a boil, and reduce the heat to medium-high. Steam for about 15 minutes, until tender. Once the yam is dried and cool enough to handle, transfer to the bowl of a food processor. Pulse until smooth. Strain the pulp through a large-mesh sieve, using a silicone spatula to press through as much as possible. Discard any solids, and gather 1 cup cooked yam.

8. **Making the yam mousse filling:** In a stainless-steel mixing bowl, using an electric handheld mixer, whisk the egg yolks with ¼ cup sugar until the mixture thickens. Set up another double boiler, and place a heatproof bowl filled with the whisked eggs on top. Beat the eggs at full speed for 4–5 minutes. Check the temperature of the eggs; they should feel warm to the touch and the mixture should fall like a ribbon of sauce when you lift the whisk. Remove from the double

boiler; add ½ teaspoon vanilla extract and ¼ teaspoon salt. Let cool to room temperature, cover with plastic wrap, and refrigerate for at least 30 minutes. In another mixing bowl, whisk the mascarpone cheese with ¼ cup sugar to soften it. Slowly add the egg mixture to the mascarpone. Mix well. Add the yam mixture. Stir until the mixture is thick but uniform. Clean your hand-held mixer in hot soapy water and finish with cold water so the blades are cold. Whip 2½ cups cold cream at low speed for 2–3 minutes until creamy and smooth. Add the remaining sugar. Increase to maximum speed and keep beating for another 2–3 minutes, until it forms soft peaks. Pour ⅓ of the whipped cream into the mascarpone cream. Mix well with a silicone spatula. Pour in the remaining whipped cream; gently fold it in to get an airy mousse.

9. **Filling the mold:** Remove the springform pan from the refrigerator. Pipe or spoon the mousse into the springform pan. Level the filling with a spatula. Plastic-wrap one more time. Place the springform pan in the freezer for at least 2–3 hours, preferably overnight.

10. **Making the chocolate glaze:** Place ¼ cup cream in a saucepan and bring to a near boil. Pour the cream over 2 ounces chocolate chips. Add 1 tablespoon honey, 1 tablespoon butter, and ½ teaspoon vanilla extract. Whisk until smooth.

11. **Assembly time:** Dip the reserved potato biscuits in the glaze, halfway. Remove any excess chocolate glaze and let the chocolate set. Run a knife around the inner wall of the springform pan. Carefully remove the pan wall. Gently unmold the cake and transfer onto a cooling rack. Decorate with the dipped potato biscuits. Allow to rest for an hour. Decorate by dusting with powdered sugar, using a fine mesh strainer.

About the Author

Jacqueline Pham is the creator of *www.phamfatale* *.com/haute-potato*, a blog that allows her to interact with other foodies who share her passion for gourmet cooking and international culture. She has experience developing, testing, and photographing recipes for food manufacturing, and has had the opportunity to cook for a Nobel laureate, several *Fortune* 100 executives, a former U.S. ambassador to the United Nations, and even a famous Hollywood actor!